Barcelona

This book explores the complex relationship between urban commons – understood as a repertoire of collective action that fosters a politics of antagonism – and the local state. It critiques the dominant neo-institutionalist and neo-Marxist perspectives for their deterministic and siloed views, as well as the insufficient attention they pay to the municipal scale. The book proposes a more nuanced, urban-based, outcome-oriented approach rooted in assemblage theory.

The analysis addresses a central question: can urban commons-local state assemblages benefit the politics of urban commons? The book argues that they can, provided they form rhizomatic assemblages. These allow urban commons to retain their self-governing autonomy, even as they lose some of their material autonomy. Conversely, it shows that assemblages can also take arborescent forms, allowing the local state to undermine the self-governing autonomy of the urban commons.

Focusing on Barcelona, the book examines how rhizomatic and arborescent assemblages are constructed, as well as the strategies that urban commons can undertake to build rhizomatic assemblages. This book is essential for scholars, policymakers, and activists interested in urban governance, commons theory and transformative politics. It provides both theoretical insights and practical tools for harnessing the dynamics of the urban commons and the local state to drive meaningful socio-political change.

Iolanda Bianchi (PhD in Political Science and PhD in Urban Planning) is an urban and political sociologist. She works in the field of urban governance, policy, and collective action. Her research focuses on the interplay between public and collective action at the urban scale and examines how this interplay can generate governance, policy, and social change to achieve more just, equitable and democratic cities. She currently holds a Ramón y Cajal Research Fellowship at the University of Barcelona. Previously, she was a Marie Skłodowska-Curie fellow at the University of Antwerp and a Juan de la Cierva fellow at the Autonomous University of Barcelona.

Built Environment City Studies

The *Built Environment City Studies* series provides researchers and academics with a detailed look at individual cities through a specific lens. These concise books delve into a case study of an international city, focusing on a key built environment topic. Written by scholars from around the world, the collection provides a library of thorough studies into trends, developments and approaches that affect our cities.

Pemba
Spontaneous Living Spaces
Corinna Del Bianco

Vienna
Still a Just City?
Edited by Yuri Kazepov and Roland Verwiebe

Havana
Mapping Lived Experiences of Urban Agriculture
Susan Fitzgerald

Seoul
Of Islands and Megastructures
Rafael Luna

Athens
A Rapidly Changing Metropolis in the European South
Edited by Thomas Maloutas

Barcelona
Urban Commons and Local State Assemblages
Iolanda Bianchi

For more information about this series, please visit: https://www.routledge.com/Built-Environment-City-Studies/book-series/BECS

To my loved ones. To my parents, Ciccio and Luisa, for their unwavering support, even without fully understanding what I do. To my partner, Massimo, my steadfast rock, for his sharp and incisive sense of critique that shaped this work. And to my daughters, Aida and Stella, for being behind every corner with the beauty of childhood.

Barcelona

Urban Commons and Local State Assemblages

Iolanda Bianchi

Routledge
Taylor & Francis Group
LONDON AND NEW YORK

First published 2025
by Routledge
4 Park Square, Milton Park, Abingdon, Oxon OX14 4RN

and by Routledge
605 Third Avenue, New York, NY 10158

Routledge is an imprint of the Taylor & Francis Group, an informa business

British Library Cataloguing-in-Publication Data
A catalogue record for this book is available from the British Library

Library of Congress Cataloging-in-Publication Data
Names: Bianchi, Iolanda author
Title: Barcelona : urban commons and local state assemblages / Iolanda Bianchi.
Description: Abingdon, Oxon ; New York, NY : Routledge, 2025. |
Series: Built environment city studies | Includes bibliographical references and index.
Identifiers: LCCN 2025003080 (print) | LCCN 2025003081 (ebook) |
ISBN 9781032500768 hardback | ISBN 9781032504421 paperback |
ISBN 9781003398493 ebook
Subjects: LCSH: Commons--Social aspects--Spain--Barcelona |
Commons--Spain--Barcelona--Government policy | Urban policy--Spain--Barcelona
Classification: LCC HD1289.S72 B373 2025 (print) | LCC HD1289.S72 (ebook) |
DDC 333.209467/2--dc23/eng/20250430
LC record available at https://lccn.loc.gov/2025003080
LC ebook record available at https://lccn.loc.gov/2025003081

ISBN: 978-1-032-50076-8 (hbk)
ISBN: 978-1-032-50442-1 (pbk)
ISBN: 978-1-003-39849-3 (ebk)

DOI: 10.4324/9781003398493

Typeset in Times New Roman
by KnowledgeWorks Global Ltd.

Contents

Acknowledgements

This book has been made possible thanks to the support received from various academic fellowships at different stages of my career. My PhD research at the University IUAV (Italy) and the Autonomous University of Barcelona (Spain), which form the basis of this book, was funded by the Italian Ministry of Education, Universities and Research (2015–2018). During my postdoctoral research, the data and theoretical framework were updated as part of the Juan de la Cierva Postdoctoral Fellowship funded by the Spanish Ministry of Science and Innovation (2019–2022). The writing of this book was completed with the support of a Marie Skłodowska-Curie Actions Seal of Excellence Fellowship funded by the Research Foundation – Flanders (2022–2023), followed by a Marie Skłodowska-Curie Actions Fellowship under the European Union's Horizon 2020 Research and Innovation Programme, Grant Agreement No. 101110202 (2023–2024), and a Ramón y Cajal Fellowship funded by the Spanish Ministry of Science and Innovation (2024–current). These fellowships provided the essential means to develop and complete this research, for which I am deeply grateful.

The writing of this book owes also much to the constant conversations and debates shared with numerous colleagues I have had the privilege to meet over the years. There are too many to name individually, but I hope each person recognises themselves in these words and knows how much I appreciate their insights and support. In particular, I am deeply grateful for the enriching exchanges and collaborations I experienced at the Institut de Govern i Polítiques Públiques of the Universitat Autònoma de Barcelona, especially with my PhD supervisor Ismael Blanco; the Università IUAV di Venezia; the Urban Studies Institute at the University of Antwerp; and, most recently, the Department of Sociology at the Universitat de Barcelona. These intellectual dialogues have profoundly shaped my thinking and have been an invaluable source of inspiration throughout the writing process. My sincere thanks to all who contributed to this journey.

1 Introduction

Situating Urban Commons-Local State Assemblages

1.1 Introduction

The book delves into the intricate dynamics that exist between the urban commons, understood as a new repertoire of collective action that develops a politics of antagonism, and the local state, understood as the ensemble of government departments, institutions, and agencies at the municipal scale. The genesis of this inquiry lies in observations that theorisations of the commons, in particular the two most relevant strands of literature, the neo-institutionalist and the neo-Marxist currents, employ a rather siloed and deterministic understanding, guided primarily by their own ideological underpinnings regarding the state's approach to shaping the politics of urban commons (Bianchi, 2022c).

Neo-institutionalists tend to see the state as a supportive institution that can help facilitate the development of commons. They see it as a necessary partner in the creation of commons and believe that it can help provide the legal framework, resources and infrastructure necessary for the commons to flourish (Iaione and Foster, 2022). Conversely, neo-Marxists see the state as a potential obstacle to the development of commons. According to neo-Marxists, the state tends to co-opt the commons by shifting the costs of social reproduction onto communities or by taming their radical potential or even destroying them (De Angelis, 2017; Stavrides, 2016). This siloed and deterministic understanding of the interaction between the commons and the state in neo-Marxist and neo-institutionalist literature is further compromised by the absence of a theorisation of the role that the municipal scale plays in this interaction.

The theoretical advances made by this book are twofold. On the one hand, it calls for a more holistic and less deterministic understanding of the interactions between urban commons and the local state. It adds nuances to the theorisations regarding the approaches that the local state can take to the urban commons, unpacking the 'approaches' into state rationalities and policy interventions. It recognises that state rationalities can be supportive, co-opting and destructive and that they can overlap and coexist; they can lead to different policy interventions that can have unpredictable effects on the political

DOI: 10.4324/9781003398493-1

action of the urban commons, which need to be studied empirically. On the other hand, this book contends that the municipal scale must be taken into account when analysing state-commons relationships. Cities are complex, dynamic environments that present ambivalent political opportunities for the development of the politics of the urban commons, but they are also characterised by a number of economic, governance and political features that may lend themselves to be exploited by urban commons to enhance their political action. This understanding, as we will explore later on in the book, opens up a window of possibilities for developing different modalities of social change at the urban level through commons-state interactions.

Beginning from the need to add some nuance to the siloed and deterministic understanding of the relationships between the urban commons and the local state, and to acknowledge the urban and local dimension of these relationships, the book presents an outcome-oriented analysis of the interplay between the urban commons and the local state, anchored in the concept of assemblages (Deleuze and Guattari, 1987). This conceptualisation stems from the recognition that in the dense context of cities, urban commons can very rarely act in a completely *autonomous* way from other institutional actors, especially the local state (Stavrides, 2016). Most of the time they are forced to have some kind of relationship with local institutions. Understanding these interactions as assemblages allows us to develop a less siloed and less deterministic view of their relationships. The analysis is motivated by an intriguing inquiry: can urban commons-local state assemblages be beneficial for the politics of the urban commons? This question serves as a starting point for examining the various ways in which relationships between urban commons and the local state can be beneficial for the politics of the urban commons. This examination makes use of another of Deleuze and Guattari's analytical devices: the distinction between rhizomatic and arborescent assemblages.

The book develops one central argument. It contends that urban commons-local state assemblages can be beneficial for the politics of the urban commons, as long as they fit together in a rhizomatic manner. In these assemblages, which are characterised by non-hierarchical and non-assimilated structures, urban commons and the local state come together in a way that allows the commons to retain their self-governing autonomy while (but not necessarily) partially losing their material autonomy. While decision-making autonomy is the ability of urban commons to define their political project and goals, material autonomy is understood as the set of financial, legal, and logistical resources that urban commons require to survive and thrive. Creating rhizomatic assemblages means that while urban commons may be dependent on the local state for material support, this relationship does not necessarily mean that they lose their ability to define the scope and goals of their transformative projects, i.e. they do not necessarily lose their capacity for self-government. In other words, the book argues that a distinction must be made between self-governing autonomy and material autonomy and that the loss of material autonomy does not necessarily lead to the loss of self-governing autonomy. The book also draws attention to the fact that urban commons-local state assemblages can sometimes take the shape of what can be called arborescent assemblages, or evolve into them. These assemblages are characterised by a hierarchical and assimilated structure, allowing the local state to undermine the self-governing autonomy of the urban commons.

The book sets its research in the city of Barcelona and examines how local state rationalities and policy interventions regarding the urban commons may affect the construction of rhizomatic and arborescent assemblages. By doing this, the book goes beyond the compartmentalised and static approaches to urban commons-local state relationships observed in the scholarly literature on the commons. Instead, it engages with the complexity and fluidity that characterises these assemblages. It challenges the notion of pregiven configurations of assemblages and examines how these configurations are built on the ground and how they often lead to outcomes that defy initial expectations based on the rationality of the local state. Furthermore, by positing the wide window of political possibilities open to the local scale, the book is also a reflection on the capacity of cities to be an initial site for the development of further socio-political transformations. The ultimate goal of the book is to explore how commons-state assemblages that take place in cities might be strategically leveraged to enhance progressive and transformative politics. This exploration strives to provide insights that are not only theoretically novel but also practically relevant for a wide array of stakeholders: local policymakers, grassroots activists, and the academic community.

The following sections of this introductory chapter will first outline the relatively recent re-emergence of urban commons in European cities and their capacity to generate political action that challenges the neoliberal order while offering alternatives in the here and now. Second, it will discuss the dominant neo-institutionalist and neo-Marxist perspectives on interactions between commons and the state, highlighting how these frameworks often overlook the complexity of such interactions and the critical role played by the municipal scale. Third, it will explore the application of assemblage theory, based on the work of Deleuze and Guattari, to interactions between urban commons and the local state, emphasising a more relational, contingent, and agency-driven understanding of these dynamics. The chapter also introduces the concepts of rhizomatic and arborescent assemblages, also drawn from Deleuze and Guattari, and applies them to urban commons and local state interactions, arguing that while arborescent assemblages impose hierarchical control and limit self-governing autonomy, rhizomatic assemblages preserve the self-governing autonomy of urban commons, thereby enhancing their politics. The chapter then sets the stage for the examination of some specific urban commons-local state assemblages by introducing Barcelona's socio-political context, the specific case studies and the methodology employed. Finally, the chapter provides an overview of the structure of the book.

1.2 An emerging political practice in European cities: the politics of the urban commons

Over the last 20 years, European cities have experienced a remarkable resurgence in urban collective mobilisation (Briata et al., 2020). This resurgence can be understood as a complex, multi-faceted phenomenon that is rooted in a variety of changing political, economic, and social conditions. However, it has mainly been interpreted as a response to the economic and social insecurities triggered by neoliberal policies and the financial crises related to them (Mayer et al., 2016). Ordinary citizens became increasingly disillusioned by rising inequalities, low wages, precarious working conditions, restrictions of tenants' and workers' rights, the privatisation and commodification of public goods and services, etc. They began to organise and mobilise in order to voice their concerns, demand change, and explore alternatives to the prevailing economic model. Beginning with the urban uprisings in Paris, Athens, and Copenhagen in 2005–2007, this collective mobilisation reached a turning point after the financial crisis of 2007–2008. In the wake of this crisis and the subsequent implementation of austerity measures, the 'movement of the squares' erupted in 2011 in many major cities across Europe: tens of thousands of people took to the streets, occupying public spaces and demanding political and economic reforms. Within this context of mobilisation, a notable phenomenon re-emerged and gained strength alongside these movements: urban commons (Varvarousis et al., 2021)

The urban commons can be considered self-managing practices of resources and services that act politically, in Laclau and Mouffe's (1978) antagonist meaning. These 'urban commons' include squatted and non-squatted social and cultural centres, housing cooperatives, workers' cooperatives, community-managed urban gardens, and consumer groups. Other, more contentious repertories, including the urban movements from which they often spring that call for more democratic and de-commodified cities (although such demands often go beyond the urban dimension) tend to enact more disruptive and conflictual politics. In contrast, the politics of urban commons is based on the everyday, i.e. on the practice of a more democratic and de-commodified pattern of urban life (Arampatzi, 2017). In other words, although the goals of urban movements and urban commons are similar, what distinguishes them is how these goals are pursued: urban movements use a demands-oriented modality while urban commons use an everyday-oriented modality (Bianchi, 2024). Rooted in the functioning of daily life, they not only critique state and market regimes but also generate alternative social relations, discourses and institutions to substitute them.

The politics of the urban commons is based on the premise that their collective social organisation can serve as a site of resistance to the neoliberal order constructed by dominant institutions, namely the state and the market. By reclaiming and collectively managing urban resources and services, communities can challenge both the logic of profit-driven market management and also that of bureaucratic state management. However, the antagonist politics of the urban commons is not only about resistance. It is also about building alternatives. By collectively managing urban resources and services, communities can create new forms of social organisation that are based on principles of cooperation, direct democracy, and reciprocity. This can lead to the creation of alternative modes of production, reproduction, distribution, and consumption that challenge the modes adopted by market and state forces. In this sense, the politics of the urban commons is not just a negative or oppositional approach to politics, but a positive and constructive one as well. Scholars have termed this type of political action as the 'everyday politics of the urban commons' (Roussos, 2019).

In this book, we share this conceptualisation of the urban commons. We consider urban commons as self-managing practices of resources and services that enact everyday politics in cities by resisting the neoliberal state-market order and by building alternative projects and disseminating alternative values (Bianchi et al., 2022). By doing this, they constitute points of political antagonism – which contribute to creating and deepening social differences (Laclau and Mouffe, 1978) – that need to be articulated between one another and with other forms of contentious politics, such as urban movements, to bring about social transformation (De Angelis, 2017).

Urban commons, and practices of self-government in general, have always existed in European cities (De Moor, 2013). Housing cooperatives, sociocultural centres, and work cooperatives have regularly represented an alternative way of conceiving urban life, one that opposes the dominant capitalist paradigm and its different urban phases. However, social movement scholars have shown that ever since the neoliberal turn of capitalism, urban commons have begun to diversify, in particular since the 2007–2008 economic recession and the implementation of austerity measures. They have steadily grown in number, and they now include practices such as community-managed urban gardens, food co-ops, and community kitchens. Indeed, several studies have shown that a plethora of these practices have re-emerged and multiplied since 2007–2008, along with subsequent urban mobilisations, and have collectively re-appropriated key urban resources and/or services to self-manage them (Cruz et al., 2017). These data confirm the role of neoliberalism, its crises and the collective need to respond to them as variables that, although they do not exhaustively explain the phenomenon, which is undoubtedly linked to structural processes that go beyond the socio-economic dimension, are important factors to consider when explaining the emergence of urban commons (Mayer et al., 2016).

In conclusion, the emergence of urban commons in European cities represents a significant shift in urban collective mobilisation. These self-managing initiatives, rooted in everyday politics, offer tangible alternatives and challenge the dominant neoliberal order based on state and market. Through social and cultural centres, housing and workers' cooperatives, community-managed urban gardens, and digital platforms, urban commons foster social change by creating and disseminating alternative values, that practices, and institutions. By connecting and collaborating with other forms of contentious politics, urban commons have the potential to trigger progressive social transformations. However, it is evident that urban commons are embedded in the socio-political context in which they act, and that their political actions can be greatly influenced by the major institutions that they theoretically seek to challenge and overcome, namely the market and the state. In this book, we focus mainly on the influence that state action, in particular local state action, can exert on the politics of the urban commons.

1.3 Urban commons-local state interactions: a siloed and deterministic understanding

Scholars consider the neo-institutionalist and neo-Marxist approaches to be the main schools of thought on the commons (Rossi and Enright, 2017). One element that these two main schools of thought share is a rather siloed and deterministic vision of the relationship between the commons and the state (Bianchi, 2022c).

The neo-Marxist analysis of commons, expounded by authors that share the understanding of the commons as points of political antagonism, often presents them as *autonomous* entities separate from the state and the market. They stress that this autonomy should be maintained in order to pursue the politics of the commons. These authors tend to be sceptical of the relationships that commons might establish with the state: they see this relationship as a path towards the inevitable destruction or co-optation of the commons (De Angelis, 2017; Stavrides, 2016). They argue that the state and the market have historically been responsible for the enclosure and privatisation of common resources, leading to the commodification of public and community goods and spaces (Midnight Notes Collective, 2001); and that this is the same tendency we are facing today in our cities (Hodkinson, 2012). One way in which the state perpetuates this destruction or co-optation of the commons is by integrating them into mainstream governance circuits through policies that provide them with material support. This includes legal frameworks, economic resources, logistical backup, and development of infrastructure (Mayer, 2013). This material support, in the same way as any other type of relationship that commons establish with the state, is seen by these authors as a process that will limit their political action.

However, it is important to recognise that this critical perspective may have limitations. By dismissing the potentially positive role of the state, and in particular the material support that it can provide them with, these authors may be overlooking the ways in which the state can enhance the politics of the commons, and may also be misunderstanding the ways in which they actually function. While it is true that the state has been implicated in the enclosure and co-optation of the commons, we cannot take this process for granted. Moreover, if it is true that one of the ways in which commons have historically been co-opted by the state is by establishing a relationship with it in order to obtain material benefits (Mayer, 2013), it is also thanks to this material support that they have been able to flourish (Huron, 2018). The rules and regulations established by the state inevitably frame the politics of the commons. In addition, financial support, development of infrastructure, and logistical support from the state can help them to grow and prosper. In conclusion, the neo-Marxist analysis of commons often overlooks the interplay between these commons and the state, in which the material benefits gained by the commons can be a tool to enhance their political action, despite the risks of co-optation.

In contrast with those who espouse the neo-Marxist perspective, another group of authors align themselves with the neo-institutionalist school of thought, influenced by the work of Ostrom (1990), and have delved into the relationship between commons and the state (Iaione and Foster, 2022). These authors do not view commons as points of political antagonism that are *autonomous* from the state and the market, but rather as alternative forms of management that can coexist with the state and the market. They emphasise the potential for collaboration and cooperation between these entities. According to them, the state can play a constructive role by providing a supportive legal framework, the necessary economic resources, and the essential infrastructure and logistical backup for the development and enhancement of commons in cities. These authors have highlighted how state involvement can contribute to the success and sustainability of commons, and how the state can be a necessary partner to help them thrive.

However, it is also important to acknowledge the limitations of this perspective. While these authors recognise the positive aspects of the relationship between commons and the state, especially in terms of obtaining the material support necessary for them to emerge and develop, they sometimes overlook the power dynamics and asymmetries that exist between them. The state, as the dominant actor, has a significant capacity to influence and control the commons. In some cases, the state can exploit its relationship with commons, established through the material support it provides, in order to advance its own agenda or co-opt the commons for political or economic purposes. This can result in the loss of the commons' antagonistic nature or even lead to their eventual destruction. Therefore, while it is important to acknowledge the neo-institutionalists' perspective that the state can play a supportive and enabling role in the politics of commons, especially by providing material support, we cannot ignore that it can also undermine them, as neo-Marxist scholars have posited.

Despite their differences, one aspect that both the neo-institutionalist and neo-Marxist approaches share is their tendency to overlook the municipal scale of commons-state interactions. When these approaches incorporate empirical evidence to support their theoretical arguments, they primarily analyse cases of commons located in urban environments. However, they do not thoroughly examine what the *urban* means for the emergence and development of urban commons (Bianchi, 2024). As many social movement scholars have stated, cities cannot merely be considered backdrops or empty canvases on which political action unfolds (Uitermark et al., 2012). Cities and political action are mutually constitutive and involve a distinctive, urban way of acting politically (Beveridge and Koch, 2019), something that imparts a unique character to the politics of the urban commons. As a consequence of not considering the particularities of the municipal scale, both neo-institutionalist and neo-Marxist approaches to analysing the relationship between commons and the state often treat the state as a monolithic entity, failing to recognise that urban commons primarily engage with the local government to meet their material needs. However, as state theorists suggest, the state cannot be seen as a unitary political organisation (Jessop, 2015). Instead, it is an ensemble of agencies, departments, and scales that may not function in a unified way; within this ensemble, the local scale in particular has specific characteristics that may be key in developing the politics of the urban commons.

In this book, we seek to overcome these limitations suffered by both the neo-Marxist and neo-institutionalist perspectives. On the one hand, we contest that the local state can adopt multiple, overlapping, and evolving approaches to the urban commons. However, we do not call them 'approaches', but rationalities, to indicate that they represent intentions that the local state has towards the urban commons, but do not determine their outcome. These rationalities may entail policy interventions that may or may not produce the expected outcomes. On the other hand, we seek to incorporate the municipal dimension into the analysis of commons-state interactions. We argue that within the complex political context that cities offer, including specific economic, governance, and political features, the local state can act as a node of disunity within the broader ensemble of state scales, providing a window of political possibilities for the politics of the commons to develop. This perspective highlights the unique role that local governments can play, offering new avenues for understanding and leveraging the potential for social change at the municipal level.

In sum, this book seeks to bridge the perspectives offered by neo-Marxist and neo-institutionalist scholars on the relationship between the urban commons and the local state, by moving beyond a dichotomous and pre-determined vision of either a relationship based on support or on co-optation and destruction. It does so by examining the municipal dimension where these relationships unfold and by arguing that local state-urban commons interactions are far more complex than what can be inferred by the ideologically driven, deterministic and siloed nature of neo-institutionalist and neo-Marxist positions. In particular, although we share the neo-Marxists' understanding of the urban commons as points of political antagonism, we show that the local state can also help enhance the politics of the urban commons. However, we do not reject the neo-Marxist perspective outright. In other words, the book will seek to develop a fuller, more nuanced understanding of the interactions between urban commons and the local state. It will do so by engaging with a powerful stream of literature in complex thinking, that of assemblage theory.

1.4 An epistemology for urban commons-local state interactions: urban commons-local state assemblages

Assemblage thinking has experienced a remarkable surge in popularity of late. Scholars across a wide range of disciplines in the social sciences are actively embracing this approach in order to understand all manner of social formations. By viewing assemblages as dynamic arrangements of heterogeneous and emergent components, which are strategically organised in specific temporal and spatial contexts, researchers have used assemblage thinking to shed light on various phenomena. Geography has employed these ideas to understand the formation of cities (McCann and Ward, 2012), sociology to understand large-scale social relations (Amelina, 2021) and political science to critically examine policy-making processes (Ureta, 2014), to name but a few applications. Scholars have drawn inspiration from the philosophical works of Gilles Deleuze and Félix Guattari. These authors were the first to put forward and use the concept of assemblage (*agencement* in French) in their book *A Thousand Plateaus* (Deleuze and Guattari, 1987).

Starting from the need to construct a theory of multiplicity, Deleuze and Guattari understand an assemblage as a dynamic configuration or arrangement of heterogeneous but autonomous elements that come together and interact in a complex social formation. These are unique formations, each with its own history, strongly influenced by the territorial, social, economic, and political context in which they develop. Crucial to this theorisation is the relational dimension of the arrangement (Savage, 2020). Assemblages are not unities: they are made up of many distinct, interconnected components that preserve their own autonomy. According to DeLanda (2016), this has two implications. First, that we cannot consider a social formation as the mere aggregate of its components; instead, this social formation must be understood in the ways in which these components act upon it and relate to each other. This means that if we consider two versions of the very same social formation, with identical components, when the components are arranged so that they interact in a different way with each other, this results in two different social formations. Second, we cannot understand the various components of the social formation as being determined by the social formation itself. This means that the different components of an assemblage can be disconnected from one assemblage and re-connected to another, where they will act in a different mode to determine that, second, social formation.

Another crucial dimension of assemblage theory is that of contingency (Baker and McGuirk, 2016). Assemblages can evolve and change. The components of an assemblage come together at particular times, in specific places and in distinct circumstances, creating a new social formation which may disappear the next day, only to be rebuilt the day after and once again broken up the following day. Assemblages, in other words, are constantly made and unmade. This means that in addition to considering the relationships and interactions between the different components of assemblages, it is important to consider the contingency of how these relationships develop and transform (Savage, 2020). That is, it is necessary to consider how a given social formation shifts, is redefined and is reconfigured according to how different components come together in diverse manners and relate to one other in varying ways, across different times and geographies. Contingency thus becomes a way of not just holding on to the here and now in the study of social formations, but also a way of thinking about flux, past and future, genealogy, and futurology (in terms of possibilities). In other words, it means looking at the mutable nature of assemblages.

The last crucial dimension of assemblage theory is that of agency (Baker and McGuirk, 2016). Assemblages are not the outcome of chance, but are made. They constantly weave and unravel, requiring a delicate and persistent effort to maintain their shape amidst ever-changing arrangements. This ongoing effort emphasises how the different components of the assemblage must put their agency to work to create the assemblage and to maintain, change, and undo it over time (Savage, 2020). The agency inherent in the components of the assemblage implies that they form strategic relationships with each other, driven by the objective of achieving specific desired effects. This does not mean that all components of the assemblage have the same degree of agency. In line with Foucault's decentralised theory of power, Deleuze and Guattari's vision sees agency, i.e. the capacity to affect the assemblage, as something that is shared among its various components, but at the same time unevenly distributed among them.

Once we understand the characteristic elements of assemblage thinking, in order to understand the specific epistemology upon which this book is based, we can apply them to the study of the assemblages under examination here, namely urban commons-local state assemblages. To rethink the interaction between these two entities as an assemblage means focusing on the relationship between them, on how it is constructed and why, and on how this relationship can influence the political objectives of each. This is done without ever forgetting that we are talking about two autonomous entities that can decide to change, modify, and end this relationship at any moment, and also that these assemblages are far from static, and transform rapidly over time. Urban commons-local state assemblages may emerge, dissolve, and resurface in response to specific social, political, and economic events, circumstances, and temporalities. This dynamic emphasises the need to consider not only the current relationships between the two components, but also how these relationships have formed and evolved in response to their location, to various contingencies and to the action of other agents. In addition, rethinking the interaction between the urban commons and the local state as an assemblage requires a focus on the persistent efforts that each component puts into the formation and modification of the assemblage. It means keeping in mind that power can be exercised by different bodies, entities, and mechanisms, including both the urban commons and the local state; at the same time, the imbalances in the distribution of this power and how it can be influenced by internal and external agents of the same assemblage need to be considered.

This epistemology associated with assemblage thinking has implications for studying the possible benefits gained by the politics of urban commons from urban commons-local state assemblages. Rethinking the interaction between these two entities as an assemblage means, first and foremost, not taking for granted the political advantages and disadvantages of this relationship, as neo-institutionalists and neo-Marxists tend to do, albeit in different ways. Neither the enhancement of the politics of the commons nor their co-optation and destruction can be expected from this relationship. Its political advantages and disadvantages will depend on how the relationship between each of its components is engendered and configured. It depends on the interaction between these two autonomous entities shifting, changing, or possibly ending, a possibility that remains open at any given moment in response to internal and external factors. It also depends on how each entity will decide to use its agency to influence this relationship, the strategic approaches it will adopt to further its own political ends, and to what effect. How will power, which is not concentrated in the hands of the local state but unevenly distributed between the local state and other politics actors, including the urban commons, affect the configuration of this assemblage?

In essence, the application of these features of assemblage thinking to the specific context of urban commons-local state assemblages provides a nuanced understanding of their intricate dynamics, one that allows us to move beyond the simplistic, siloed, and deterministic understanding pursued by the neo-institutionalists and neo-Marxists that has been described above. It paints a vivid picture of how urban commons-local state formations can evolve, interact, and transform within the urban landscape to achieve specific political benefits that are far from predetermined. This is because these assemblages are affected by their relationships, by contingency, and by the unevenly distributed but strategic agency of their components. This book takes this assumption as a starting point, namely that we cannot take for granted that the relationship between the urban commons and the local state will unfold according to a predetermined pattern. In exploring the complexity of this relationship, we will focus on how it can be shaped to be politically beneficial to the politics of the commons. It is argued that this is achieved through the construction of rhizomatic urban commons-local state assemblages. In the following section, we will outline the characteristics of these assemblages and how they differ from the arborescent assemblages.

However, before going any further, an important point needs to be stressed. Perhaps it seems somewhat paradoxical that, within a theory of complexity and multiplicity, here we are considering an assemblage that is composed of only two elements, the urban commons and the local state, when we know that an assemblage can be made up of an extensive series of components: political actors, events, scales, circumscriptions, laws, and so on. We would therefore like to specify that although in this book it is urban commons-local state assemblages that are being discussed, this definition does not aim to fully represent these assemblages but is used more as a rhetorical device, a synecdoche, a part for the whole. The aim is to help the reader better appreciate the relationship between the main components of the assemblage that we are interested in analysing. Our focus on the relationship between these two components does not, however, mean that the other possible components of assemblage are to be ignored, quite the contrary. They will also be carefully considered in the analysis, particularly the municipal dimension, but filtered through the lens of the relationship between the urban commons and the local state that we are interested in analysing, in order to understand their political impact (or lack thereof) on that relationship.

1.5 Rhizomatic and arborescent assemblages: enhancing the politics of the urban commons

Assemblage theory has gained ground in academia, penetrating, as we have seen, the discourses and analyses of many disciplines. However, in the work of Deleuze and Guattari, in addition to the idea of assemblages, we find many other conceptual elements which, although equally powerful and evocative, have not enjoyed as much popularity in scholarly debates. In particular, *A Thousand Plateaus* (1987), a book that represents one of the milestones in assemblage theory, contains many other concepts that can be useful in refining assemblage theory. These concepts include molecular and molar, territorialisation and deterritorialisation, or, for example, the idea of rhizome and tree. All of these notions are conceptual pairs that the two French philosophers use extensively in their work, but which have not found widespread application in contemporary theories. In this book, we will make use one of these conceptual pairs, that of tree-rhizome, to advance the main claims of the book. As we have already suggested, we argue that urban commons-local state assemblages can enhance the politics of the urban commons, but only if they take the form of a rhizomatic assemblage. What this means exactly is explained in the next few paragraphs of this section.

In the philosophical discourse of Deleuze and Guattari, the concept of the rhizome is juxtaposed with that of the root and the tree, drawing inspiration from botanical terms. In botany, a rhizome is a subterranean stem that extends horizontally; conversely, a tree exhibits a hierarchical structure, with branching systems growing from a central trunk. Deleuze and Guattari employ these metaphors to illustrate contrasting modes of organisation, functioning and thought. The arborescent structure of a tree adheres to a vertical growth pattern that features trunks and branches that form hierarchies, with specific points and nodes of connection created between the components. The rhizomatic model contrasts with this: it follows a decentralised configuration where each element can connect to other elements directly, and is devoid of predefined reference points (Woods et al., 2013). This decentralised growth reflects the botanical particularity of the rhizome, in which the parts interconnect without requiring hierarchical pathways. In botanical terms, examples of rhizomatic assemblages include irises, spider plants, ginger, bamboo, and lotus flowers, while examples of arborescent assemblages include oak, pine or apple trees. In organisational terms, the functioning of the Internet or a Linux system could be compared to a rhizome, while the functioning of a corporation or a bureaucratic administration might be compared to a tree (Gehman et al., 2022).

In the light of our theorisation and argument, the most significant features of these two types of assemblage – the rhizome and the tree – are the modalities through which these two types of assemblage connect structurally and the modalities through which the desires and identities of the components are governed. Let us proceed in order. The way in which an arborescent assemblage is structured is through a fixed hierarchy, which has a rigid organisation and straight connections (Woods et al., 2013). The orderly top-down organisation of an arborescent assemblage has nodes and points through which new components of the assemblage can be grafted, but which must follow these predetermined paths. The rhizome is structured differently. Here, connections can be created between any of the components, irrespective of the routes preferred by a dominant component. Rhizomatic assemblages facilitate connections between different elements, while avoiding fixed patterns and centralised cores. There are no established positions in the rhizome like those in a tree, only lines that can be moulded and modified (Gehman et al., 2022). In other words, the rhizomatic assemblage is 'anti-hierarchy', because, unlike an arborescent assemblage, it does not articulate or create hierarchies among its components.

Arborescent assemblages subsume the desire and identities of the many components under the principal one through 'coding'. The notion of codification appears in an arborescent assemblage when one of the components seizes power or when a corresponding process of assimilation occurs, in order for its shape to be held together. The component that perpetuates this process limits, assimilates, consumes, and absorbs the desires and identities of the others. In contrast, in rhizomatic assemblages, desires and identities are maintained and self-governed. They are allowed to persist and coexist and are subject to dynamic negotiation but never eradicated or erased. A rhizome does not allow itself to be over-coded. There is no imitation, no resemblance in a rhizomatic assemblage, but an explosion of heterogeneous elements (Gehman et al., 2022). As Deleuze and Guattari (1987, p. 25) put it: ‘The tree is filiation, but the rhizome is alliance, uniquely alliance’. In other words, the rhizomatic assemblage is ‘anti-assimilation’ because it does not subsume or over-code components in the way the arborescent assemblage does.

As suggested by Guareschi (2017), Deleuze and Guattari’s use of the rhizome-tree conceptual pair, along with other pairings such as molecular-molar, territorialisation- deterritorialisation, might appear paradoxical within their theory of multiplicity, which aims to transcend dichotomies. However, escaping dualism is not as simple as introducing additional terms or transforming two terms into three or four. For these authors, breaking free from dichotomy is not achieved through quantitative augmentation, but through a process of becoming. Dualism emerges when two concepts unequivocally divide the world, such as the contrast between the concrete and the abstract: the concrete is not abstract, and vice versa. This does not apply to Deleuze and Guattari’s conceptual pairings: the tree can transform itself into a rhizome, and the rhizome, in turn, is susceptible to stiffening, closing up, becoming rooted, or disappearing due to excessive dispersion. In this way, the status of tree or rhizome is not fixed but is forged in an ongoing, processual contingency – the characteristics of contingency and agency observed earlier re-emerge here. Rhizome and tree, as with other conceptual pairs, are not meant to be dualistic opposites, alternative and mutually exclusive, but rather mixed statuses in which one type of assemblage can have characteristics of the other and/or mutate into the other. In this context, as Guarini elucidates, the rhizome and tree function as evaluation coefficients, against which we can assess the status of each assemblage.

What does it mean to apply these conceptualisations to urban commons-local state assemblages, and what implications can the construction of either type of assemblage have for the development of the politics of the urban commons? In the context of this book, this conceptual pair reflects two different types of relationships that can be established between the local state and the urban commons. The creation of an arborescent assemblage implies that the local state hierarchises the relationship with the urban commons and imposes its own points of connection, be they events, circumstances, policies, discourses, etc. In this vertical structuring of the relationship between these two actors, as the neo-Marxist literature suggests, the local state tends to co-opt the urban commons, and sometimes even destroys them. In other words, the local state tends to subsume their transformative projects by codifying them according to its own ways of acting, seeing and thinking. This codification of the urban commons mainly takes place by the local state implementing policies that, by providing material support, harness them and mould them so that they resemble the bureaucratised and market-oriented logic. This harnessing by the local state aims to control the urban commons' governance of their desires and identity, i.e. to limit their capacity to decide on the objectives and scope of their transformative projects. Ultimately, it means limiting both their material and their self-governing autonomy.

Conversely, creating a rhizomatic urban commons-local state assemblage means creating a relationship between these two actors that is as horizontal as possible. This relationship is not based on domination but on a linear interconnection in which not only the local state but also the urban commons define their points of connection. In this type of assemblage, the transformative projects of the urban commons are not shaped along the lines often used by the local state, which tend towards a bureaucratised and market-oriented logic. This does not mean that urban commons do not participate in public policies and actions that provide them with material support. They generally need to do so for reasons of necessity, survival, and recognition (although a few strictly autonomous cases do exist). Instead, it means that the urban commons, while participating in policies that provide them with material support, manage to govern their desires and their identities relatively autonomously, i.e. they keep hold of their capacity to decide on the objectives and scope of their transformative projects. In other words, a rhizomatic urban commons-local state assemblage is one in which urban commons, while receiving material support from the local state and thus losing their material autonomy, manage to maintain their self-governing autonomy.

The conceptual pair of rhizomatic and arborescent urban commons-local state assemblages, like Deleuze and Guattari's conceptual pair, should not be seen as dichotomous, clear-cut and totalising. As we will see in the cases analysed in the book, the reality is far more complex than the binary, simplistic, and reductive visions sometimes presented by neo-institutionalists and neo-Marxists, in which urban commons are either supported or else co-opted and destroyed by the local state. Pure effects are difficult, if not impossible, to find. Even in the case of rhizomatic and arborescent urban commons-local state assemblages, we must see them as terms that allow us to assess the primary status of each assemblage, which will be imperfect and hybrid. As well as seeing these assemblages as hybridised and imperfect, we need to consider the possibility of mutation. This means that we should be attentive to any movement, any *line of flight* that – under the agency of each main component and the other so-called secondary components, laws, events, and circumstances – can lead to the status of each assemblage being modified. In other words, in this book, we will devote our attention to the hybrid and changing nature of rhizomatic and arborescent urban commons-local state assemblages. In particular, we will be attentive to how rhizomatic assemblages can be maintained, defended, and sustained over time so that urban commons do not lose their self-governing autonomy and are able to perform their political action.

1.6 Researching urban commons-local state assemblages: Barcelona, case studies, and methods

Our examination of urban commons-local state assemblages is situated within the context of Barcelona, the capital of the autonomous region of Catalonia in Spain. The choice of Barcelona is strategically significant, and the case studies are rooted in the city's distinct socio-political context. Firstly, Barcelona boasts a longstanding tradition of self-organisation. This originated in the early 1900s and is deeply ingrained in a prevalent anarcho-collectivist culture. This tradition, eclipsed during the Franco regime and the early democratic years in Spain, resurfaced in the late 1980s with the emergence of squatting and cooperative movements. The financial crisis of 2007–2008, along with subsequent anti-austerity mobilisations in 2011 (known in Spain as the 15M or the *Indignados* movement), catalysed the resurgence of urban commons throughout Catalonia, particularly in cities like Barcelona. These now encompass a spectrum of initiatives, ranging from urban agriculture to community-led housing (Cruz et al., 2017). Secondly, after the democratic shift, the city has predominantly been governed by left-wing coalitions, except for the 2011–2015 term when a right-wing administration held power. These left-wing coalitions have fostered a form of collaborative local state-urban commons assemblage regime, based on informal dialogues with urban collectives, and the existence of formal participatory spaces and policies to support the many civic initiatives in the city. Furthermore, Barcelona was one of the epicentres of the so-called Spanish New Municipalist wave (Russell, 2019). In 2015, a series of New Municipalist candidacies, composed of left-wing parties and activists, ran in the municipal elections, winning in 15 major Spanish cities. Notably, the Barcelona en Comú (BComú) party clinched a victory in the local elections, with Ada Colau, a former activist leader of the anti-eviction movement, taking on the role of mayor (Blanco et al., 2020). BComú has always had close links with local social movements and has committed to supporting urban commons. Through its election victories, the self-organising values and demands of the new wave of urban commons managed to enter the local state debate, and helped produce commons-sympathetic policies (Bianchi et al., 2022), such as funding for social and solidarity economy initiatives, the promotion of social housing through housing cooperative schemes, and better legal footing for community-managed public spaces and facilities.

Barcelona offers a compelling backdrop for examining urban commons-local state assemblages, yet this study acknowledges the inherent constraints of focusing exclusively on this city. Every city, including Barcelona, bears its own distinctive blend of historical, socio-political, and cultural elements that influence its governance structures and collective action dynamics. Thus, outcomes drawn from this particular context might not seamlessly translate to other urban settings, particularly those with very different socio-political or cultural landscapes. Barcelona's exceptional political history, characterised by its specific local state-urban commons assemblage regime, the presence of robust civic participation evident in the myriad urban commons there, and the New Municipalist politics embodied by BComú, has shaped a unique urban milieu. These particular circumstances might not exist in other cities or may be very different. Nonetheless, this does not mean that the insights gleaned from this research cannot be applied to other urban contexts. In particularly, the central argument of the book – advocating the construction of rhizomatic assemblages between urban commons and the local state to enhance the effectiveness of urban commons' political action – is relevant across diverse settings. The specific nature of the Barcelona context lies in the possibilities it offers for developing such assemblages, predominantly due to Barcelona's relatively favourable circumstances in this regard, making the development of rhizomatic assemblages more attainable.

Our primary focus is the city of Barcelona, which serves as the central case study. Within this context, a qualitative-interpretative approach is used to undertake a subsequent comparative analysis of sub-cases. These sub-cases involve distinct urban commons-local state assemblages that emerged within the city in the same period: the Puigcerdà informal settlement and the Can Batlló sociocultural centre. The Puigcerdà informal settlement, established in 2011 by a group of predominantly sub-Saharan immigrants, aimed to provide shelter for the group and allow its members to engage in informal economic activities for sustenance. Meanwhile, the Can Batlló sociocultural centre originated in 2011 through the mobilisation of local residents, with the intention of providing cultural facilities in their neighbourhood. The case selection was guided by two critical criteria: the cases needed to occur concurrently but involve different social groups, forming two distinct types of urban commons-local state assemblages. The Puigcerdà case represents a predominately arborescent assemblage, while the Can Batlló represents a predominantly rhizomatic assemblage. The deliberate choice of two concurring but contrasting assemblages, each forming a different type of urban commons, allows us to examine the varying political agency exercised by the same local state (governed by same political parties) in shaping these assemblages, as well as the potential of each urban commons' agency to influence them. This comparative analysis aims to illustrate the circumstances which may foster the formation of rhizomatic and arborescent assemblages, always bearing in mind the imperfect nature of each assemblage and how it may evolve.

The research presented in this book embodies the culmination of several years' work, encompassing my doctoral studies and early postdoctoral research. It is important to note that this is not just a version of my doctoral thesis (Bianchi, 2018), but that it integrates theoretical considerations and fieldwork carried out in subsequent years (Bianchi, 2022a, 2022b, 2022c; Bianchi et al., 2022). Nevertheless, it is correct to recognise my thesis as the main source of information for the empirical part of the work. This empirical section, as mentioned above, focuses on studying the formation and consolidation of state-commons assemblage regimes in general in the city of Barcelona since the beginning of the century, and closely examines two urban commons-local state assemblages, tracing their evolution from their inception in 2011 until 2021. The research took place primarily between March 2016 and June 2017 (during my doctoral studies), but additional analysis was conducted between January and June 2021 (during my postdoctoral research) to secure updated data for both case studies. The data collection process relied on the triangulation of different sources of evidence. Notably, this encompassed document analysis, involving local newspaper articles, press releases issued by Barcelona City Council, and policy reports. Moreover, the research encompassed 25 semi-structured interviews, involving participants from grassroots welfare initiatives, municipal officials and politicians, activists, and experts on the subject matter. These interviews were recorded and transcribed manually, with subsequent analysis facilitated by the Nvivo10 software for data coding and cross-case comparison.

The rest of the book is structured as follows. Chapter 2 explores neo-Marxist and neo-institutionalist theories of the commons, looking at the different ways they conceptualise the commons and understand the relationship between the commons and the state, as well as the way that both currents neglect the municipal scale in their theorisations. The chapter then develops the analytical framework of the book, which seeks to bridge the two perspectives of the relationship between the commons and the state by adopting a more flexible and less deterministic approach, while also integrating the municipal scale into the analysis. Chapter 3 is dedicated to the case study of Barcelona and explores the evolution of the local state-urban commons assemblage regimes in the city from the early 1900s to the present, with particular attention given to the political developments that occurred after the 2007–2008 financial crisis: the rise of urban commons and the arrival of the New Municipalist movement. Chapters 4 and 5 focus on the presentation of the two case studies: on the one hand, the construction of what appears to be a predominantly rhizomatic assemblage between the local state and the Can Batlló urban commons; and on the other, what appears to be a predominantly arborescent assemblage between the local state and the Puigcerdà urban commons. The chapters examine how the rationalities and political interventions of the local state affect the creation and evolution of these assemblages, and how the urban commons use them (or not) to develop their political action. Chapter 6 summarises the main arguments made in the book, presents what might be the three main strategies for urban commons to enhance their political action through local state-commons assemblages, and outlines avenues for future research.

References

Amelina A (2021) Theorizing large-scale societal relations through the conceptual lens of cross-border assemblages. *Current Sociology*, 69(3): 352–371. DOI: 10.1177/0011392120931145.

Arampatzi A (2017) Contentious spatialities in an era of austerity: Everyday politics and 'struggle communities' in Athens, Greece. *Political Geography* 60: 47–56. DOI: 10.1016/j.polgeo.2017.03.010.

Baker T and McGuirk P (2016) Assemblage thinking as methodology: Commitments and practices for critical policy research. *Territory, Politics, Governance* 5(4): 425–442. DOI: 10.1080/21622671.2016.1231631.

Beveridge R and Koch P (2019) Urban everyday politics: Politicising practices and the transformation of the here and now. *Environment and Planning D: Society and Space* 37(1): 142–157. DOI: 10.1177/0263775818805487.

Bianchi I (2018) *In, Against, Beyond and Through the State. Limits and Possibilities of Urban Commons in Barcelona.* Barcelona: Universitat Autònoma de Barcelona; Venezia: Università IUAV di Venezia.

Bianchi I (2022a) Empowering policies for grassroots welfare initiatives: Blending social innovation and commons theory. *European Urban and Regional Studies* 30(2): 107–120. DOI: 10.1177/09697764221129532.

Bianchi I (2022b) The autonomy of urban Commons' reproduction in relation to the local state: Between material and decision-making autonomy. *Partecipazione & Conflitto* 15(2): 370–389. DOI: 10.1285/i20356609v15i2p370.

Bianchi I (2022c) The local state's repertoires of governance strategies for the urban commons: Nuancing current perspectives. *Environment and Planning C: Politics and Space* 40(8): 1784–1800. DOI: 10.1177/23996544221108333.

Bianchi I (2024) The everyday politics of the urban commons: Ambivalent political possibilities in the dialectical, evolving and selective urban context. In: Hamel P and Domaradzka A (eds) *Handbook of Urban Social Movement.* London: Edward Elgar Publishing, pp. 284–300.

Bianchi I, Pera M, Calvet-Mir L, et al. (2022) Urban commons and the local state: Co-production between enhancement and co-optation. *Territory, Politics, Governance* 12(9): 1333–1352. DOI: 10.1080/21622671.2022.2108491.

Blanco I, Salazar Y and Bianchi I. (2020) Urban governance and political change under a radical left government: The case of Barcelona. *Journal of Urban Affairs*, 42(1), 18–38. DOI: 10.1080/07352166.2018.1559648.

Briata P, Colomb C and Mayer M (2020) Bridging across difference in contemporary (urban) social movements: Territory as a catalyst. *Territory, Politics, Governance* 8(4): 451–460. DOI: 10.1080/21622671.2020.1799851.

Cruz H, Martínez Moreno R and Blanco I (2017) Crisis, urban segregation and social innovation in Catalonia. *Partecipazione e Conflitto* 10(1): 221–245. DOI: 10.1285/i20356609v10i1p221.

De Angelis M (2017) *Omnia Sunt Communia*. London: Zed Books.

DeLanda M (2016) *Assemblage Theory*. Edinburgh: Edinburgh University Press.

Deleuze G and Guattari F (1987) *A Thousand Plateaus: Capitalism and Schizophrenia*. Chicago: University of Minnesota Press.

De Moor T (2013) *Homo Cooperans. Institution for Collective Action and the Compassionate Society*. Utrecht: Universiteit Utrecht.

Gehman J, Sharma G and Beveridge A (2022) Theorizing institutional entrepreneuring: Arborescent and rhizomatic assembling. *Organization Studies* 43(2): 289–310. DOI: 10.1177/01708406211044893

Guareschi M (2017) Saggio Introduttivo. In Deleuze and Guattari, Mille Piani Capitalismo e Schizofrenia. Napoli: Orthotes Editrice

Hodkinson S (2012) The new 'urban' enclosures. *City* 16(5): 500–518. DOI: 10.1080/13604813.2012.709403.

Huron A (2018) *Carving out the Commons: Tenant Organizing and Housing Cooperatives in*. Washington, D.C. Minneapolis, MN: University of Minnesota Press.

Iaione C and Foster SR (2022) *Co-Cities: Innovative Transitions toward Just and Self-Sustaining Communities*. Cambridge, Massachusetts: The MIT Press.

Jessop B (2015) *The State: Past, Present, Future*. Cambridge: Polity Press.

Laclau E and Mouffe C (1978) *Hegemony and Socialist Strategy: Towards a Radical Democratic Politics*. London: Verso.

Mayer M (2013) First world urban activism: Beyond austerity urbanism and creative city politics. *City* 17(1): 5–19. DOI: 10.1080/13604813.2013.757417.

Mayer M, Thörn C and Thörn H (2016) *Urban Uprisings: Challenging Neoliberal Urbanism in Europe*. London: Pelgrave.

McCann E and Ward K (2012) Assembling urbanism: Following policies and 'Studying Through' the sites and situations of policy making. *Environment and Planning A: Economy and Space* 42–51. DOI: 10.1068/a44178.

Midnight Notes Collective (2001) The new enclosures. *The Commoner* 2: 1–15.

Ostrom E (1990) *Governing the Commons*. Cambridge: Cambridge University Press.

Rossi U and Enright T (2017) Ambivalence of the urban commons. In: Jonas A, Miller B, Ward K, et al. (eds) *Handbook on Spaces of Urban Politics*. New York: Routledge, pp. 77–88.

Roussos K (2019) Grassroots collective action within and beyond institutional and state solutions: The (re-)politicization of everyday life in crisis-ridden Greece. *Social Movement Studies* 18(3): 265–283. DOI: 10.1080/14742837.2018.1562330.

Russell B (2019) Beyond the local trap: New municipalism and the rise of the fearless cities. *Antipode* 51(3): 989–1010. DOI: 10.1111/anti.12520.

Savage G (2020) What is policy assemblage? *Territory, Politics, Governance* 8(3): 319–335. DOI: 10.1080/21622671.2018.1559760.

Stavrides S (2016) *Common Space: The City as Commons*. London: Zed Books.

Uitermark J, Nicholls W and Loopmans M (2012) Cities and social movements: Theorizing beyond the right to the City. *Environment and Planning A* 44(12): 2546–2554. DOI: 10.1068/a44301.

Ureta S (2014) Policy assemblages: Proposing an alternative conceptual framework to study public action. *Policy Studies* 35(3): 303–318. DOI: 10.1080/01442872.2013.875150.

Varvarousis A, Asara V and Akbulut B (2021) Commons: A social outcome of the movement of the squares. *Social Movement Studies* 20(3): 292–311. DOI: 10.1080/14742837.2020.1793753.

Woods M, Anderson J, Guilbert S and Watkin S (2013) Rhizomic radicalism and arborescent advocacy: A Deleuzo-Guattarian reading of rural protest. *Environment and Planning D: Society and Space* 31(3): 434–450. DOI: 10.1068/d14909.

2 Beyond Neo-Marxist and Neo-Institutionalist Dichotomies

Commons-State Assemblages in the Urban Context

2.1 Introduction

While commons used to be a widespread form of organising in pre-capitalist societies, the advent of industrial capitalism led to their marginalisation, as the new economic system prioritised private property, market-based exchange, and state control (for a comprehensive understanding of why this marginalisation occurred, see Bianchi, 2018a). This shift relegated the commons to the periphery of economic and social organisation in the 18th century and first half of the 19th century (Mattei, 2011). In recent decades, however, there has been a resurgence of interest in the commons, driven by both neo-institutionalist and neo-Marxist scholarship. These two scholarly approaches have contrasting understandings of the commons, their potential roles, and, in particular, the political possibilities offered by commons-state assemblages. These understandings are rooted primarily in the ideological positioning of each current rather than in empirical evidence. Moreover, although these scholarly traditions often analyse commons-state assemblages that unfold at the municipal level, neither actually analyse how this particular scale affects the political possibilities of these potential assemblages.

In this section, we will examine neo-institutionalist and neo-Marxist theories with the aim of bridging and nuancing their perspectives regarding the construction of commons-state assemblages, and of filling the gap regarding the municipal dimension of this scholarship. In the first part, we will introduce the neo-institutionalist and neo-Marxist traditions of scholarship on the commons. Second, we will present their siloed and deterministic understandings of state approaches in the emergence and development of commons-state assemblages. Third, we will develop our more nuanced perspective, based on a more holistic and less deterministic approach to analysing commons-state assemblages. In the second part of the chapter, we will incorporate the specificities of the municipal scale into the analysis of commons-state assemblages, demonstrating the political ambivalences offered by the urban dimension and the window of political possibilities offered by the local state. This dual approach will provide us with a more comprehensive framework

DOI: 10.4324/9781003398493-2

for understanding and analysing the potential and challenges of the politics of urban commons-local state assemblages in contemporary cities.

2.2 The re-emergence of the commons: the neo-institutionalist and the neo-Marxist perspectives

Of the two intellectual traditions discussed in this book in terms of their treatment of the commons, it was undoubtedly the neo-institutionalist tradition, particularly through the contributions of the Nobel prize winner in economics, Elinor Ostrom (1990), that reignited interest in this form of resource management and governance. Ostrom's work aimed to contest prevailing theories of collective action, such as Olson's 'logic of collective action' (Olson, 1971), Dawes' 'prisoner's dilemma game' (Dawes, 1973), and Hardin's 'tragedy of the commons' (Hardin, 1968), that were also theories that justified the marginalisation of the commons. Despite their differences, all these models painted a bleak picture of individuals unable to prevent the degradation of the commons. In her landmark book, *Governing the Commons* (1990), which was the culmination of decades of research on this topic, Ostrom challenged these perspectives. Firstly, she contended that the popularity of these models stemmed from their simplicity, which offered policymakers easily predictable outcomes and thus encouraged straightforward actions such as privatisation or state control of commons. Moreover, Ostrom argued that these models relied on overly simplistic assumptions, such as constant levels of lack of communication among individuals, as well as their inability to establish rules and institutions and to manage the information available. Through a comprehensive review of numerous case studies of various commons, Ostrom demonstrated that individuals do indeed possess the capacity for communication, collective decision-making, institution building, and information processing. In essence, she showed that communities could successfully organise and manage shared resources collectively, in the form of commons, thereby challenging traditional models of collective action.

In her early work, Ostrom focused on a specific category of commons resources known as Common-Pool Resources (CPRs). According to neoclassical economics, CPRs differ from other type of resources – public, private, and club resources – in terms of two main features: high exclusion costs, meaning that it is difficult but not impossible to prevent people from using the resource, and high subtractability, meaning that any portion taken by one user reduces the amount available for others. Examples of CPRs include productive assets such as irrigation systems, alpine meadows, underground water reservoirs, and nearshore fisheries. By analysing all these cases, Ostrom formulated a new theory of collective action that identified key design principles that would allow group management of CPRs to be successful. These principles are as follows: (1) the community that uses the resource must be well defined;

(2) the rules on the use of the CPR must respect the local conditions in which it is located; (3) individuals who use the CPR must be able to participate in decision-making processes and in changing the rules; (4) there must be people who check if the rules are respected or not; (5) people who do not respect the rules are likely to be sanctioned; (6) there must be spaces for discussion in order to resolve the conflicts that arise; (7) external governmental authorities must recognise the rights of the community to set up their own institutions; and (8) a nested structure needs to be in place in larger systems (Ostrom, 1990).

One crucial aspect of Ostrom's understanding of the commons, which also aligns with post-Marxist views, is the imperative of self-government. In her third design principle, referred to as 'the collective choice arrangement', she emphasises that those impacted by the operational rules of CPRs must be involved in creating, modifying, and enforcing these rules. Hence, participation and horizontal governance are key elements. Ostrom rejected the idea of top-down rules, particularly ones imposed by external institutions, instead advocating a community's ability to self-determine their governing protocols. However, unlike some post-Marxist scholars, Ostrom never used this model of self-government to question the existing capitalist system. As pointed out by scholars such as Dardot and Laval (2015), Ostrom's approach is fundamentally liberal and fits within the framework of neoclassical economics. In her work, she argues that these self-governing communities possess high levels of social capital and the ability to self-organise, but she sees their actions as guided by cost-benefit rationalities, rooted in a profit-driven paradigm. In this model, resources are inputs for production processes or commodities to be sold on the market (Federici and Caffentzis, 2013). Therefore, in Ostrom's view, individuals, when collaboratively managing a resource, essentially operate as entrepreneurs who are fully integrated into the capitalist system. For her, thus, the commons are not a source of antagonistic political agency, but a mere management strategy that complements the state and the market's governance models, all within the capitalist system.

Later on in her career, Ostrom expanded her research focus from natural to immaterial resources, focusing particularly on what she termed 'Knowledge Commons' (KCs). Her understanding of knowledge encompassed a broad range of intellectual assets, from indigenous wisdom to scientific research, although her primary focus was on scholarly and scientific information (Hess and Ostrom, 2007). Thus, while she maintained her neo-institutional methodological approach, positing that the analytical framework used for CPRs could also be applied to the study of KCs, the resources under scrutiny had shifted noticeably from CPRs. Traditionally, knowledge, due to its intangible nature, has been considered a public good: it is something accessible to everyone and non-subtractable and covers areas such as ideas and scientific discoveries. However, the advent of digital technologies such as digital libraries, repositories, community archives, and open-access journals has transformed how this resource is structured and managed. As a result, many digital communities now manage knowledge much like they would manage CPRs. This shift to studying KCs marked a significant evolution in Ostrom's thought and departed from the naturalistic assumptions of commons rooted in neoclassical economic theory. She came to recognise that what define a commons are not solely the inherent qualities of the resource itself, but also the management style adopted by a collective of individuals. However, even with this shift, her viewpoint remained fundamentally a liberal one. For Ostrom, whether dealing with KCs or CPRs, these resources represented another form of collective management that could coexist alongside state and market governance models, all within the capitalist system. In contrast, a very different interpretation of the commons and their political potential is offered by neo-Marxist theorists.

Neo-Marxist interest in the commons began to gain prominence in the 1970s, coinciding with the implementation of the neoliberal projects. These scholars began to scrutinise the historical underpinnings of capitalist development, particularly focusing on the phenomenon of 'enclosures'. In classical Marxist theory, enclosures play a critical role in what is termed 'primitive accumulation' (Marx, 1867). This was the process through which communities and individuals were dispossessed of their means of production, primarily arable land, during the 15th and 16th centuries. This dispossession facilitated the creation of a labour force comprising individuals who were compelled to sell their labour, and thereby became subjects of exploitation. In addition to Marx, scholars such as Polanyi (1944) have also discussed this historical shift in order to emphasise that the emergence of capitalism was not a result of entrepreneurial genius, but instead emerged from a violent process of appropriating a resource – arable land – that had formerly been held in common. According to classical Marxist understanding, however, the process of enclosure itself occurred during a specific historical period, aligning with the genesis of capitalism and concluding once the capitalist system had been established.

Scholars within the neo-Marxist tradition, such as Caffentzis, De Angelis, and Federici, have challenged the traditional understanding of enclosures by de-contextualising and de-historicising this process. They argue that enclosures are not confined to a specific historical period culminating in the genesis of capitalism. Instead, they see enclosures as an ongoing, discontinuous mechanism that underpins the entire history of capitalism and enables its continuous reproduction (De Angelis, 2017; Federici and Caffentzis, 2013). With the rise of neoliberalism, this mechanism has been reinvigorated in an especially aggressive manner, leading to what have been called 'new enclosures' (Midnight Notes Collective, 2001). New enclosures, which involve the privatisation and commodification of resources that should be considered commons, occur both in the Global North – particularly impacting public goods and services – and in the Global South, where they target land cultivated by local communities. These processes are facilitated by collaboration between state and market authorities. Similarly, Harvey describes this phenomenon as 'accumulation by dispossession', a process in which new assets are privatised and commodified with the intention of making them available at low cost or even zero cost, allowing capitalists to seize them for profit (Harvey, 2010).

In summary, the notion of enclosure, along with its modern-day manifestations, has equipped neo-Marxist scholars with the analytical tools to comprehend how, for the capitalist system to survive, it fundamentally relies on the privatisation and commodification of the commons, i.e. goods belonging *de facto* to local communities (such as arable land), national communities (such as public goods and services), and global communities (such as water and seas), even though these communities are not considered *de jure* owners. From this conceptualisation, the commons emerged as an alternative and opposing paradigm to enclosure and to the development of capitalism (Bianchi, 2018b). In more recent times, in fact, the very neo-Marxist scholars who have updated the concept of enclosure are also the ones who see the commons as a new mechanism that enables marginalised and exploited populations to carve out a new route towards emancipation from capitalism.

In theoretical terms, neo-Marxist scholars have developed multiple interpretations of the commons: as a mode of collective production and reproduction that represents the possibility of regaining control of the means of production and reproduction and extricating lives from the market and the state (De Angelis, 2017; Federici, 2018); as a political and social instrument for the direct fulfilment of fundamental rights, creating institutional forms that go beyond the accumulation of wealth and power of the state and the market (Mattei, 2011); and as collective forms of organising production and distributing wealth and value that aim to displace market forces and the accumulation of capital (Harvey, 2012). Without wishing to minimise the nuances of each one of the perspectives, a summary based on Harvey's definition might offer a unifying viewpoint. Harvey characterises the commons as 'a social relation between a particular self-defined social group and those aspects of its actually existing or yet-to-be-created social and/or physical environment deemed crucial to its life and livelihood' (Harvey, 2012, p. 73).

The crucial nature of the social relations between the community and the resource highlights the political dimension of the commons (Bianchi, 2018b). This means that the group is not just acting jointly to manage the communal resource but is also as a political actor that, by recognising that the resource is crucial for its survival, makes a series of demands: that it not be used according to the economic logic of capitalism, i.e. a profit-making logic; that it not be governed according to capitalism's preferred governance system, i.e. representative democracy; and that it not be structured according to the capitalist mode of social relations, i.e. competitive social relations. Therefore, the crucial nature of these social relations compels the community involved to develop a model that operates based on the economic logic of use-value, to establish a governance system rooted in direct democracy, and to cultivate social relations grounded in reciprocity. The construction of social relations between the collective and the resource means that the commons do not only include collectively managed resources, such as urban gardens, cultural hubs, art centres, housing and workers' cooperatives, but also include resources such as water and healthcare, which are managed by other institutions, but for which the community is campaigning for a more equitable, more democratic, and more de-commodified form of management (Bianchi, 2018b). Thus, for neo-Marxist scholars, the commons are a source of antagonist political agency, offering an alternative to both state and market governance models and embodying a tool for progressive social transformation.

In sum, neo-institutionalist and neo-Marxist perspectives on the commons represent different intellectual traditions. While Elinor Ostrom's neo-institutionalist framework reignited interest in the commons by challenging traditional theories of collective action, it remained largely within a liberal economic paradigm, seeing the commons as a management strategy that was compatible with state and market models of governance. Conversely, neo-Marxist scholars have reinterpreted the concept of enclosure as an ongoing capitalist process and have positioned the commons as a radical alternative to both state and market models of governance. They see the commons not just as a management tool, but as a political instrument for resisting capitalist enclosures and building a more just, democratic society. As one might imagine, these two divergent traditions also have different understandings of the approaches taken by the state in the construction of commons-state assemblages.

2.3 The commons and the state: the neo-institutionalist and the neo-Marxist perspectives

The neo-institutionalist tradition might appear to have a very ambiguous view of the state's approach to the construction of commons-state assemblages. The work of Ostrom has been criticised for seemingly adopting an 'adversarial' stance towards the state, viewing it as an actor that might play a destructive role in an assemblage with the commons (van Laerhoven et al., 2020). Ostrom's design principles, seen earlier, which are intended to outline the features of enduring and successful commons, have been a focal point in this discussion. Her seventh principle posits that 'the rights of appropriators to design their own institutions are not challenged by external government authorities', a guideline that has been misconstrued as an anti-state sentiment (Mansbridge, 2014). After all, this is also the design principle that, together with her third principle, most closely aligns Ostrom's thinking with that of the neo-Marxist authors, in the sense that it says that commons need to be managed by the community without the interference of external authorities, such as the state.

Yet, a more nuanced reading of Ostrom's oeuvre requires us to examine her eighth principle, formulated for managing large-scale and more complex commons. This principle posits that 'nested' structures need to be in place in larger governance systems. Although Ostrom does not refer directly to the state in this principle, but speaks merely of nested structures, in reality these nested structures could include the state and its territorial units, whether national or regional. Indeed, at one point in her book, Ostrom (1990, p. 212) recognises that commons do not exist in isolation and that especially in the case of commons that are not located in remote places, such as ones in cities, the state may have a fundamental contribution to make in the creation of commons or in the resolution of their conflicts. As she argues, 'regional and national governments can play a positive role in providing facilities to enhance the capacity of local appropriators to engage in effective institutional design' (Ostrom, 1990, p. 212). This should be done while always respecting, in accordance with Principle number 3, the right of communities to ultimately define their own rules.

This is also the main message of another of Ostrom's central concepts: 'polycentrism'. Developed in the context of her study of the management of public services and resources in urban settings, polycentrism indicates a form of governance that is performed by multiple, and sometimes overlapping, centres of decision-making. Each operates with some degree of autonomy, but they are all nested within multiple jurisdictional levels (Ostrom et al., 1961). As work in the neo-institutionalist field evolved, Ostrom and her peers began to use the term 'polycentric' either synonymously with, or in relation to, the idea of 'nested' governance, as outlined in Ostrom's eighth design principle for successful commons. This notion of 'nested' governance structures, in fact, aligns well with polycentrism, as it underscores the importance of having local, regional, and even national governance mechanisms that are integrated and mutually reinforcing. These layers could range from community-based organisations and local government units to state agencies and international bodies, all making their unique contributions yet fulfilling interconnected roles in the management of public services and resources.

In sum, while a more nuanced reading of Ostrom's work suggests that in her conceptual framework the state can adopt a supportive approach in assemblages with the commons, it is worth noting that she does not place this idea at the forefront of her theory-building regarding the commons. Other scholars in the neo-institutionalist tradition have highlighted how her work somewhat overlooks this idea, pointing out that Ostrom focuses more on the capabilities of groups of individuals in rule-making and enforcement when managing commons (Anthony and Campbell, 2011), in line with her neo-institutionalist perspective. In other words, although the state may provide support when creating assemblages with commons, it is not a particularly crucial or key element of her argument, which aims to demonstrate the capacity of people to self-organise, and thereby debunks Olson's collective action myth and Hardin's tragedy of the commons.

The shift towards a more robust inclusion of the supportive approaches of the state in neo-institutionalist commons theory is notably evident in urban law and governance scholarship, inspired by Ostrom's work, whose main representatives are Foster and Iaione. These authors have translated Ostrom's thinking into the dense and complex urban context. Firstly, by analysing Park Conservancies, neighbourhood foot patrols, community gardens, and Business Improvement Districts in the US, they have highlighted that urban commons depend, to varying degrees, on the support or enabling of local authorities (Foster, 2011). This support helps them to overcome obstacles to collective action and/or to sustain it over time. Secondly, they have defined a set of principles for enduring and successful urban commons, just as Ostrom did for CPRs. Their Principle number 2 clearly recognises the role of the state in facilitating the emergence and development of the urban commons. In their vision, the state's promotion of the urban commons is part of a new polycentric approach to city governance in which the provision and management of goods and services by groups of citizens should acquire a central role, and should follow principles of subsidiarity and cooperation (Foster and Iaione, 2019).

State support for the urban commons, the two authors argue, should not be sporadic and haphazard. It should take the form of a concrete urban policy that materially supports the commons on a permanent basis, through a favourable legal framework and the provision of resources, both economic and property resources. In their book *Co-cities* (Iaione and Foster, 2022), in which they condense a decade of research on the topic based on extensive empirical analysis carried out in over 200 cities worldwide, they examine different policies aimed at supporting urban commons. Among these policies, they study the Regulation for the Care and Regeneration of the Urban Commons in Bologna and the Citizen Assets Programme in Barcelona (which we also comment on later in this book). They also examine policies that support a community-governed broadband network in New York and the co-governance of community assets in Baton Rouge, as well as broader commons-inspired governance programmes carried out in some Italian cities, such as Ravenna and Turin. Their analysis shows that the collaboration established between urban commons and state authorities, especially local governments, together with other urban actors, such as educational institutions and businesses, facilitates the creation and development of commons. In their vision, the state's support of commons is part of a new polycentric approach to city governance that they call co-governance.

Co-governance emphasises a collaborative partnership occurring between state institutions and communities in the emergence and development of urban commons. This model recognises that while grassroots efforts and citizen-led initiatives are essential, they often require the backing of state mechanisms to address diverse challenges and ensure their long-term viability. Administrative support can help navigate bureaucratic hurdles, financial backing can provide necessary resources for development and maintenance, and logistical assistance can enhance the efficiency and effectiveness of operations. By advocating for co-governance, Foster and Iaione highlight the intertwined relationship between state and community actors in the emergence and development of urban commons. This approach not only leverages the strengths of community-driven efforts but also integrates the state's capacity to facilitate and enhance these efforts, which the authors say creates a more robust and flexible governance framework. The success of urban commons, therefore, hinges on this cooperative dynamic, where both the state and the commons work together towards their effective management.

In summary, while early neo-institutionalist theories led by Ostrom may have seemed to sideline the state's role in forming assemblages with commons, subsequent scholarship has clarified this oversight. In this literature, the state is now increasingly recognised as an enabler, a partner, and even a crucial element in the polycentric governance of commons, particularly in urban settings. This shift is significant as it clarifies Ostrom's understanding of commons-state relationships, allowing for a collaborative model that integrates the notion of polycentricity and the nested structure she proposed. In doing so, this literature illustrates the supportive approach that can be adopted by the state in its assemblages with commons. However, this literature does not examine how the state can also adopt less supportive roles when building commons-state assemblages, something that neo-Marxist scholars do consider.

The neo-Marxist literature on commons offers a slightly more nuanced and complex view of the state's approaches when assembling with commons, including discussions on its dynamic and changing nature. It provides a critical lens through which the contentious relationship between state power and collective management can be understood. According to key proponents of neo-Marxist theory, the state, in its efforts to accommodate the interests of capital, employs two primary approaches in its assemblages with commons: the adversarial role and the co-opting role. The adversarial approach aims to destroy or significantly undermine commons, while the co-opting role seeks to take them over by incorporating them into existing power structures. These approaches are not mutually exclusive but form integral components of state actions within neo-Marxist theory. Over time, they can alternate or overlap depending on specific socio-political circumstances, though individual scholars tend to emphasise one approach over the other in their analyses.

The adversarial approach positions the state as a destroyer of commons. Hardt and Negri (2009) characterise the state primarily as an antagonistic institution, placing it at the forefront of what they term the 'capture and expropriation of the commons'. This adversarial approach manifests in various mechanisms, including the privatisation and commodification of common resources and services, aligning with David Harvey's concept of 'accumulation by dispossession'. In a similar vein, Mattei (2011) argues that the centralising force of the state tends to shrink commons or make them disappear altogether, reinforcing the private property-state dichotomy. Critical urban scholars have provided evidence for this adversarial approach. Bresnihan and Byrne's (2015) analysis of independent cultural spaces in Dublin, which serve as critical sites for community engagement and artistic expression, reveals how state intervention, often resulting in eviction or closure, poses a significant constraint to the development of urban commons. Similarly, Di Feliciantonio's (2017) examination of urban squats in Rome documents the implementation of repressive measures taken by city councils and other state institutions, which frequently culminate in violent evictions.

Conversely, the co-opting approach perceives the state as a manipulator of commons. This approach, particularly relevant when commons engage with the state to satisfy their material needs, operates through two main logics: the economic and the political. De Angelis (2013) provides the theoretical underpinnings for the economic logic of co-optation, arguing that capitalism has reached an 'impasse' in its economic feasibility. In this context, commons emerge as an ideal 'fix' to address this impasse by displacing the cost of social reproduction onto communities worldwide. This displacement often involves expecting communities to self-manage resources and services that were previously provided by the state, but to do so with limited state support and resources. When De Angelis (2013) discusses co-optation strategies, he highlights the example of New Labour in the UK, which mobilised local groups under the attractive call of empowering communities to manage public services. Commons saw this call as an opportunity to access state resources: both economic resources and infrastructure. However, since these resources were often limited and underfunded, they did not allow commons to develop properly, leaving them to operate in precarious, exploitative conditions. This strategy effectively outsourced state responsibilities to local volunteers and community groups, masking the state's retreat from public service provision.

The political dimension of the co-opting approach draws heavily on post-Foucauldian studies. This perspective argues that the state operates according to a specific governmental rationality (Stavrides, 2016). To implement this rationality, the state deploys a range of techniques to regulate, control, and discipline collectives, with a particular focus on potentially subversive groups such as commons. These techniques, which are often deployed when commons and the state interact to meet the material needs of commons (such as negotiating property leases or applying for funding), often involve socio-spatial control mechanisms designed to tame and normalise commons projects, ensuring they do not deviate from the established political and economic order. In their study of community-managed cultural centres in Barcelona, Pera and Bianchi (2022) show how such centres, which often have to negotiate with the city council to receive funding and organise their cultural activities, frequently have their antagonistic potential undermined. The city council employs a panoply of norms and bureaucratic procedures as technologies of power to depoliticise their actions, thus curbing the centres' capacity for dissent.

Importantly, the economic and political logics of co-optation frequently operate in tandem, reinforcing each other's effects. Bianchi's (2018b) analysis of the 'Regulation for Urban Commons' in Bologna offers a case in point, showing how this framework simultaneously exploits the voluntary labour of commoners for public interest activities while quashing their more radical demands. This dual approach ensures that commons remain within manageable limits, serving state interests rather than challenging them.

In sum, neo-Marxist perspectives emphasise the adversarial and co-opting approaches of the state in its assemblages with the commons and highlight the complex and often contradictory nature of state interventions that can shift from one approach to the other or adopt both simultaneously. These perspectives show how the state, exploiting the commons' need for material support, can act both as a suppressor and a manipulator of commons, employing strategies that either dismantle or co-opt them to serve broader capitalist interests. In this way, the neo-Marxist scholarship underscores the critical impact of the state's various approaches in building commons-state assemblages. However, because they primarily view the state as an adversarial force, unlike the neo-institutionalists, they often downplay or overlook the state's potentially supportive approach when building commons-state assemblages.

2.4 Bridging the two perspectives: towards a more nuanced understanding of state-commons interactions

Both the neo-institutionalist and neo-Marxist perspectives on the commons acknowledge one or more approach that the state may adopt when forming state-commons assemblages, but these perspectives suffer from certain limitations. Firstly, they tend to adopt a relatively static understanding of the state. The state is often portrayed either as a repressive or co-opting force aligned with capitalist interests, or as an entity that can support commons. It is true that the neo-Marxist perspective is more nuanced in that it takes into account the evolving and changing nature of the state, allowing for a shift from co-optation to destruction. However, it still does not fully consider the supportive approaches that the state may adopt. This siloed portrayal fails to capture the dynamic and multifaceted nature of the state, which can simultaneously, or over time, exhibit supportive, repressive, and co-opting tendencies depending on the socio-political context and the urban commons in question (Bianchi, 2022a).

Secondly, these perspectives often focus on the approach that the state takes within commons-state assemblages, presupposing that these approaches will inevitably produce outcomes that are aligned with that approach: if the state is supportive, the commons are supported; if the state is co-opting, the commons are co-opted. These perspectives fail to critically assess the actual impact of these approaches on the commons. This limits our understanding of the capacity of commons to navigate and potentially subvert the state's approaches, as well as the unpredictable outcomes that may arise from such interactions. In this way, the inherent complexity and variability of these dynamics are not acknowledged. By failing to consider the real consequences of commons-state interactions, there is a risk of adopting a reductive view of the political possibilities, potentially underestimating the opportunities for building rhizomatic commons-local state assemblages, as well as not properly considering the risks and circumstances that might lead to the formation of arborescent ones.

To address these shortcomings, it is crucial to adopt a more fluid and outcome-oriented framework to studying commons-state assemblages. This book rejects the notion of the state as a static entity that uniformly applies a fixed approach in its interactions with the commons. Instead, it sees the state as a political actor driven by different rationalities, corresponding to the approaches delineated by neo-Marxist and neo-institutionalist theories: supporting, co-opting, or destroying. These rationalities, which represent the underlying logic that guides local state action and can be found in both right-wing and left-wing governments, may evolve over time within the same government and between governments, or may coexist within a single administration, depending on the changing political, social, and economic contexts, as well as the specific urban commons in question. Furthermore, these rationalities can lead to policy interventions that yield unpredictable outcomes for the politics of the commons, outcomes that do not necessarily align with the state's adopted rationality, depending on the agency of the commons and the socio-political context.

For instance, a local state governed by a right-wing administration may adopt a co-opting rationality towards certain commons. However, this rationality, driven by the need to tame their radical potential, could result in policy interventions that make material concessions to those urban commons – such as grants, property, and so forth – that actually enable the commons to enhance their political action, creating rhizomatic assemblages in which the commons retain their self-governing autonomy despite receiving material support from the state. Nevertheless, this approach could also pose a significant risk to the commons, as they might gradually lose their decision-making autonomy and be subsumed by the demands, expectations, and bureaucratic logic of the state. This process of absorption could lead to the commons' original objectives being diluted or redirected so that they align more closely with state priorities, ultimately resulting in them being co-opted.

Additionally, the rationalities of a state, even when governed by the same administration, may evolve and change depending on shifting political circumstances. For example, the state might decide to withdraw material concessions that had previously been granted. In such a scenario, the very survival of the commons could be jeopardised, forcing them to shift their focus from their political action to addressing their own survival. This redirection of energy and resources could weaken their capacity to pursue their original goals, thereby diluting their political impact. Furthermore, the same administration might choose to adopt a supportive rationality towards one commons – with an unpredictable outcome – while simultaneously implementing a destructive rationality towards another commons that is perceived as more radical and challenging. This dual approach can create a contradictory landscape where certain commons are allowed to exist and other are not.

All these rationalities and the resulting policy interventions may or may not shift when the state is governed by left-wing administrations. These governments might also adopt co-opting, destructive, or supportive rationalities, each with outcomes that remain uncertain and highly contingent upon the specific conditions that either facilitate or hinder the creation of rhizomatic assemblages. Even a supportive rationality, which is more likely but not guaranteed under a left-wing government, if not carefully designed, could paradoxically lead to the co-optation of the commons. Policies that are intended to promote the political action of the commons through the creation of rhizomatic state-commons assemblages might inadvertently cause the commons to be subsumed by the demands, expectations, and bureaucratic logic of the state.

In other words, the state's rationality is neither singular nor fixed; instead, rationalities are multiple and can change or coexist over time and across different contexts. These multiple, evolving and overlapping rationalities can result in a variety of policy interventions, whose effects on the political capacity of the commons and their potential to form rhizomatic or arborescent assemblages cannot be predetermined. This nuanced perspective highlights the multifaceted and contradictory nature of state action, as well as the inherent unpredictability in the relationship between the commons and the state, where different rationalities may produce policy interventions with unintended consequences, either facilitating or hindering the creation of rhizomatic assemblages.

By adopting this nuanced perspective, based on a more fluid and outcome-oriented approach, we aim to foster a more comprehensive and empirically based understanding of how the state can shape the politics of commons, ensuring that the analysis reflects the complexities of state-commons assemblages. This approach involves a close examination of the state's multiple, evolving and coexisting rationalities and its respective policy interventions in influencing the politics of the commons, to understand how, and under what conditions, it might facilitate the creation of rhizomatic or arborescent assemblages. Furthermore, this approach aims to foster dialogue between different theoretical perspectives. By bridging the divide between neo-institutionalist and neo-Marxist viewpoints, we strive to develop a more integrated understanding that facilitates an accurate assessment of the conditions under which the politics of the commons can flourish, as well as determining the strategies that commons can employ to navigate and leverage state interventions effectively.

2.5 The urban dimension of the commons: the ambivalent political possibilities of the urban context

One aspect that neo-institutionalist and neo-Marxist approaches have in common is their tendency to overlook the municipal scale of commons-state assemblages, both in terms of the urban nature of the urban commons and the local dimension of the municipal scale. Even Iaione and Foster, who focus their analysis on the municipal level, actually provide little theoretical insight into the distinctively municipal dimension of this scale. To address this under-theorisation of the municipal dimension, we examine how three key urban processes interact with the politics of the commons. These processes are urban capital accumulation, urban social relations, and urban power configurations. By analysing how each of these processes intersects with and shapes the politics of the urban commons, we can gain a more comprehensive understanding of the unique dynamics at play in urban environments. As demonstrated in our analysis below, the urban context offers ambivalent possibilities for the politics of the urban commons, potentially enhancing them but also sometimes threatening them (Bianchi, 2024). This approach shifts our understanding from viewing the city as a mere backdrop for commons-state assemblages to recognising cities as integral components of such assemblages.

The first aspect that, in our view, characterises the *urban* nature of urban commons is reflected in the specific capital accumulation processes that are developed in cities. Urban capital accumulation processes involve the investment of capital in urban settings to generate profit, especially through real estate. These processes began to emerge forcefully in the 1970s, with the neoliberal turn of capitalism, in a period in which traditional industrial production was insufficient for capital accumulation (Harvey, 2010). Key neoliberal urban accumulation processes include the privatisation of urban public spaces, the privatisation and outsourcing of welfare services, the gentrification and regeneration of low-rent and inner-city neighbourhoods, and the financialisation of housing. These processes, often referred to as urban enclosures (Hodkinson, 2012), aim to channel city resources and land to generate profit, leading to the displacement and segregation of poorer urban populations. The implementation of these neoliberal urban accumulation processes gives rise to ambivalent political possibilities for the emergence and development of the urban commons.

Critical scholars have widely demonstrated how, when the effects of neoliberal urban accumulation processes become pervasive in a city, the urban context becomes a stage on which to organise and challenge them through different repertories of collective action (Castells, 1983). These repertories include the urban commons. As already mentioned, the urban commons began to develop with the implementation of the neoliberal project and became especially pervasive in the aftermath of the 2007–2008 economic recession. This does not mean that the urban commons emerged exclusively because of the deepening contradictions of the neoliberal urban accumulation process. However, it cannot be ignored that urban commons have emerged and proliferated precisely when these contradictions became more evident and their effects more severe (Arampatzi, 2018). Scholars who focus on the spatial effects of neoliberal urban accumulation highlight that the 2007–2008 recession temporarily halted urban speculation, leaving many spaces derelict. These spaces were re-appropriated by urban commons and included self-managed gardens, squatted sociocultural centres, and collectively managed public squares. Their emergence fostered a growing desire for alternative urban spaces and increased political demands for more equitable urban development (Rossini and Bianchi, 2020). Additionally, urban commons such as soup kitchens, time banks, and migrant-led housing squats emerged in response to the severe social impacts of the recession and provided a means of survival for marginalised groups while putting forward new ways of urban living (Arampatzi, 2018).

However, the neoliberal urban accumulation process often hinders the survival and expansion of urban commons, both directly and indirectly. Direct hindrances include the deliberate destruction of urban commons by economic and political elites (spaces that were re-appropriated during the 2007–2008 economic recession, such as self-managed urban gardens, squatted sociocultural centres, etc. were particularly targeted). These spaces are often forcibly dismantled when economic activity resumes and private-led redevelopment projects target these plots (Tornaghi, 2017). Indirect hindrances stem from the intensification of neoliberal urban accumulation processes, making it extremely difficult for urban commons to access and maintain spaces in the city. Real estate pressures and soaring rental and purchase prices in most European cities (Rolnik and Hirschhorn, 2019) pose significant challenges for initiatives such as sociocultural centres, food co-ops, time banks, or housing cooperatives. Many of these initiatives, particularly ones in their infancy, struggle to find affordable spaces. Consequently, both direct and indirect obstacles contribute to the scarcity of urban commons, especially in areas that are attractive to real estate investors, such as inner-city areas targeted for gentrification and mass tourism.

The second aspect that, in our view, characterises the *urban* nature of urban commons is reflected in the specific social relations that are produced in cities. Urban social relationships are influenced by several factors, which include density, diversity, and social differentiation. The city is where diverse individuals, in terms of class, gender, ethnicity, etc. – i.e., diverse subjectivities – come together and live in close quarters with one another. This experience is mediated by the socio-spatial effects of the neoliberal urban accumulation process, such as displacement and segregation, which lead to different political responses in each subjectivity. These characteristics give rise to ambivalent political possibilities for the emergence and development of the urban commons.

Firstly, the characteristics of urban environments facilitate the emergence of urban commons by bringing together diverse subjectivities. Cities provide the public space necessary for these encounters (Merrifield, 2012); here, diverse individuals meet, share resources, communicate, and exchange goods and ideas. This interaction is not random but leads to the forging of collective identities that mediate experiences of displacement and segregation, transforming individual claims into collective claims and demands (Miller and Nicholls, 2013). It is in this sense that Hardt and Negri (2009) argue that if in the Fordist era the factory was the place of the working class, now this space is the city, since production has gone beyond the boundaries of the factory to spread throughout the whole urban fabric. But urban commons are unique forms of collective action. They not only involve the meeting of diverse subjectivities and the development of collective social relations but also their collective management. These practices teach these subjectivities to self-govern, transmit ideas, and build shared norms that allow resources to be managed collectively according to principles of reciprocity, use-value, and participatory democracy.

Nevertheless, empirical studies on urban commons also highlight the challenges of creating and maintaining these practices among diverse groups, referred to as 'strangers' by Huron (2015). The primary challenge is for members to work across their differences and to find a common language while respecting multiplicity. Huron (2018) illustrates this with the example of a housing co-op in Washington D.C., where Spanish-speaking Central Americans, Amharic-speaking Ethiopians, and English-speaking African Americans held meetings in all three languages, an arduous process that eventually led to the co-op's creation. Differences can also arise from the diverging interests each group has towards the resource, often shaped by the social differentiation that has previously been discussed. For instance, a vacant plot might be seen by some as an opportunity for local organic food production, while others might view it as a potential public community space (Kip, 2015). These challenges call for the mediation of not only cultural differences but also of the disparities produced by urban neoliberal accumulation processes. Such difficulties can lead to exclusionary practices within urban commons, where homogeneous groups dominate, reinforcing urban segregation rather than creating alternatives to capitalism (Stavrides, 2016).

Last but not least, a key element that characterises the urban nature of the commons is how urban power configurations are developed in cities. Although there are various perspectives on how power is exercised at the local level – upheld primarily by groups of pluralists, elitists, and Marxists – the local state undoubtedly remains a crucial element in the exercise of power. Due to the importance that the local state acquires in the theorisation and development of this book, in the following section, it will be discussed in detail.

2.6 Incorporating the urban dimension of the state: the political opportunities offered by the local state

The local state, like the other processes that influence the politics of the urban commons, can offer them ambivalent political possibilities (Bianchi, 2024). The hypothesis of this book bridges neo-Marxist and neo-institutionalist literature and contends that we cannot merely understand the local state as an ideologically driven form of government moved solely by one type of rationality - be it support, co-optation, or destruction - and the corresponding policy intervention towards the urban commons. Instead, all these rationalities and policy interventions are ones that can be adopted by the local state, and they can follow one other in time and space and can also overlap in time and space. There is therefore no single rationality or policy intervention that prevails within the local state; it must be analysed with all its contradictions, compromises, and incompleteness (Jessop, 2015). However, in light of the study of the politics of the urban commons and how this can be enhanced, it is worth considering the specificities of the local state, in order to understand how they can be strategically exploited by urban commons when forming urban commons-local state assemblages. The local state is part of the larger state apparatus, which is in any case embedded in a capitalist society, and therefore tends to promote capitalist development (Jessop, 2015). However, what we argue in this book is that the local state is characterised by a set of financial, governance and political specificities – openness to material resources, to participation, and to radical positionings – making it a unique entity that the urban commons might be able to exploit more easily to enhance their political action. We shall now examine how.

Before discussing what is specific to the local state and how this can be exploited by the urban commons, it is important to highlight the significance this scale of government has acquired more recently. Its newfound importance is part of a general process of restructuring and rescaling state power that was initiated around the 1970s; this encompassed upward rescaling, outward rescaling, and downward rescaling (Brenner, 2004). Upward rescaling refers to the transfer of state powers and responsibilities to higher levels of governance, such as supranational entities such as the European Union. Outward rescaling involves the delegation of state functions to external actors, such as private firms or non-governmental organisations, often through privatisation and outsourcing. Downward rescaling denotes the decentralisation of power to lower levels of government, such as regional or municipal administrations, enhancing their regulatory and policy capacities. This includes legislative powers, fiscal responsibilities, and administrative duties. As a result of this rescaling, regional and local governments increasingly gained autonomy. Local governments, in particular, became crucial actors in fostering economic development through policies that were designed to attract capital investment, to implement new urban planning schemes, and to control public spaces. Additionally, as part of the process of welfare subsidiarisation, local governments began to manage public services, playing a key role in areas such as care, culture, migration, and housing.

The significance acquired by the local state is thanks to it being the government level that has the material resources that urban commons most frequently seek to use (something also recognised by neo-institutionalist scholars), and which they are sometimes obliged to use to meet their material needs. Indeed, the local state possesses most of the economic, logistical, infrastructure, and policy resources to meet these needs. In terms of economic resources, the local state can provide direct funding, grants, and subsidies to support the activities of commons. Additionally, it can facilitate access to low-interest loans or provide tax incentives for initiatives that align with public interests. These economic resources can be used by urban commons to financially sustain their activities, especially when they begin their activities or when the commons in question are not designed to generate profit. In terms of infrastructure, the local state often controls significant physical assets that can be made available to the urban commons (Bianchi, 2022b). These include public spaces such as parks, real estate, and vacant lots that can be used by urban commons to host their activities, especially in cities where real estate speculation, gentrification processes, and mass tourism make it difficult to rent or buy property at market prices. In terms of logistical support, the local state can assist with the logistics of running urban commons by providing essential services such as technical support for specific activities run in public spaces or events, as well as waste collection and water and energy supplies. In terms of policy resources, the local state can enact commons-sympathetic policies that support the emergence and development of urban commons (Bianchi et al., 2022). This kind of policy support may be crucial for the development of some urban commons in the city, such as housing cooperatives or cultural centres, that might struggle to take off without a favourable policy and regulatory environment in place.

In addition to providing material resources, the local state is also characterised by being more open to instigating participatory processes. We do not wish to fall into the 'local trap' by asserting that the city is a more democratic unit of governance compared to other units (Purcell, 2006). However, it must be acknowledged that the local state is often the level of government where so-called democratic innovations are most often implemented (Falanga, 2024). Examples include participatory budgeting, the recent climate assemblies, and the more established participatory processes for various urban planning projects. While being aware of the taming and co-opting potential that these spaces can acquire, with the risk of local public authorities tending to simply involve less radical groups to legitimise their public policies and thereby create a post-political consensus (Bianchi, 2018b), we believe that all these participatory spaces can be exploited by the urban commons to enhance their political action. If they are aware of the co-optation risks, urban commons can engage in these participatory spaces to create a more favourable legal environment for their initiatives or to ensure that their needs are taken into account, and a material base is provided for their activities. It is precisely through this reasoned and critical participation, a form of participation marked by conflict, that urban commons can succeed in altering the trajectory of participatory processes shaped by technocracy and the creation of consensus, in order to use them in their favour (De Tullio and Micciarielli, forthcoming).

Last but not least, there is another layer of openness that characterises the local scale, which we refer to as being open to radical positionings. This possible openness of the local state to consider radical ideas, similar to its openness to participation, should not be interpreted dogmatically. However, it is important to note that within the capitalism-prone state ensemble, the local state is the level of government where radical left-wing groups have managed to gain power or, at the very least, have secured seats on municipal councils. The New Municipalist movement, which emerged in Spain in 2015 and also took hold in other European contexts such as Italy, France, and Croatia, exemplifies this empowerment of left-wing coalitions that bring together leftist parties with activists and social movement groups (Russell, 2019). The reasons for this rise to power are multifaceted and must be understood in their structural dimension: the pronounced capitalist effects within urban contexts, the smaller constituencies of local governance that may be less influenced by media and large corporations, and the geographical particularities of the state-capitalist nexus. These factors must also be contextualised at the European and national levels, considering the dramatic effects of the 2007–2008 crisis, austerity policies, and the unprecedented social mobilisation these events triggered, exemplified by the *Indignados* movement in Spain (see Chapter 3). Furthermore, these reasons need to be contextualised at the local level, taking into account the political trajectory and specificities of each context, including its tradition of left-wing politics, history of movements and activism, the depth of the economic crisis there, and the capacity to mobilise and build a political alternative at the party level. Beyond the reasons for this victory, it is evident that urban social movements, including urban commons, view the local scale as a more accessible entry point for gaining power and developing a radical political agenda, reviving a long-standing yet highly relevant tradition of municipal socialism. This openness to radical positionings is another factor that can be exploited by urban commons to enhance their political action. Once New Municipalist movements gain some form of governmental power, urban commons, by maintaining close contact with politicians aligned to their causes or public officers, can push to secure and protect resources, create spaces for contentious participation, and help define legal and policy frameworks that favour their development.

In sum, the local state, with its unique openness to participatory processes, to radical positionings, and to material resources, offers fertile ground for urban commons to enhance their political action when forming urban commons-local state assemblages. Despite the ambivalent political possibilities inherent in the urban scale, the hypothesis of this book suggests that the local state may be a level of government that can be more easily exploited by the urban commons in order to enhance their political action. By doing so, urban commons can navigate and influence the local state's tendencies to promote capitalist development, turning these specificities to their advantage. However, for urban commons to effectively enhance their political action, they must form rhizomatic assemblages with the local state. This involves creating non-hierarchical and non-assimilated structures, where urban commons and the local state come together in a way that allows the commons to retain their self-governing autonomy, while possibly (but not necessarily) losing some of their material autonomy.

2.7 Conclusion

In this chapter, we have explored the two primary strands of literature on the commons – namely neo-institutionalist and neo-Marxist theories – to move beyond their siloed and deterministic perspectives regarding the state's approaches when forming assemblages with the commons. We have proposed a more nuanced framework to unpack the general term 'approaches' into what we define as state rationalities and policy interventions. We recognise that the state may adopt multiple, evolving, and coexisting rationalities when engaging with commons – supportive, co-opting, and destructive – which can lead to various policy interventions that, in turn, may produce a range of unpredictable outcomes for the politics of the commons. Additionally, we have incorporated the specificities of the municipal scale into our analysis of commons-state assemblages, demonstrating how the urban dimension – characterised by specific processes of capital accumulation, social relations, and power configurations – offers ambivalent political possibilities for enhancing the politics of the urban commons. Despite these ambivalences, the context of the municipal scale presents significant political opportunities for the urban commons. In this context, urban commons can leverage the specificities of the local state – such as openness to participation, radical positionings and material resources – to bolster their political action. For this political action to be genuinely effective, however, urban commons-local state assemblages must take on a rhizomatic form, in which the commons maintain their self-governing autonomy. We will operationalise this theoretical and analytical framework in the next chapter by examining the case of Barcelona.

References

Anthony DL and Campbell JL (2011) States, social capital and cooperation: Looking back on governing the commons. *International Journal of the Commons* 5: 284–302. DOI: 10.18352/ijc.250.

Arampatzi A (2018) Constructing solidarity as resistive and creative agency in austerity Greece. *Comparative European Politics* 16(1): 50–66. DOI: 10.1057/s41295-016-0071-9.

Bianchi I (2018a) *In, Against, Beyond and Through the State. Limits and Possibilities of Urban Commons in Barcelona*. Universitat Autònoma de Barcelona; Università IUAV di Venezia.

Bianchi I (2018b) The post-political meaning of the concept of commons: The regulation of the urban commons in Bologna. *Space and Polity* 22(3): 287–306. DOI: 10.1080/13562576.2018.1505492.

Bianchi I (2022a) The local state's repertoires of governance strategies for the urban commons: Nuancing current perspectives. *Environment and Planning C: Politics and Space* 40(8): 1784–1800. DOI: 10.1177/23996544221108333.

Bianchi I (2022b) The autonomy of urban Commons' reproduction in relation to the local state: Between material and decision-making autonomy. *Partecipazione & Conflitto* 15(2): 370–389. DOI: 10.1285/i20356609v15i2p370.

Bianchi I (2024) The everyday politics of the urban commons: Ambivalent political possibilities in the dialectical, evolving and selective urban context. In: Hamel P and Domaradzka A (eds) *Handbook of Urban Social Movements*. London: Edward Elgar Publishing, pp. 284–300.

Bianchi I, Pera M, Calvet-Mir L, et al. (2022) Urban commons and the local state: Co-production between enhancement and Co-optation. *Territory, Politics, Governance* 12(9): 1333–1352. DOI: 10.1080/21622671.2022.2108491.

Brenner N (2004) *New State Spaces: Urban Governance and the Rescaling of Statehood*. Oxford: Oxford University Press.

Bresnihan P and Byrne M (2015) Escape into the city: Everyday practices of commoning and the production of urban space in Dublin. *Antipode* 47(1): 36–54. DOI: 10.1111/anti.12105.

Castells M (1983) *The City and the Grassroots: A Cross-Cultural Theory of Urban Social Movements*. Berkeley: University of California Press.

Dardot P and Laval C (2015) *Común*. Ensayo Sobre La Revolución Del Siglo XXI. Barcelona: Gedisa.

Dawes RM (1973) The commons dilemma game: A N-Person mixed motive game with a dominating strategy for defection. *ORI Research Bulletin* 13: 1–12.

De Angelis M (2013) Does capital need a commons fix? *Ephemera: Theory and Politics in Organizations* 13(3): 603–615.

De Angelis M (2017) *Omnia Sunt Communia*. London: Zed Books.

Di Feliciantonio C (2017) Spaces of the expelled as spaces of the urban commons? Analysing the re-emergence of squatting initiatives in Rome. *International Journal of Urban and Regional Research* 41(5): 708–725. DOI: 10.1111/1468-2427.12513.

Falanga R (2024) Democratic innovations: Is the local scale (still) the ideal laboratory for democracy? *Local Government Studies* 50(6): 1052–1061. DOI: 10.1080/03003930.2024.2407010.

Federici S (2018) *Re-Enchanting the World: Feminism and the Politics of the Commons*. Oakland: PM Press.
Federici S and Caffentzis G (2013) Commons against and beyond capitalism. *Upping the Anti: A Journal of Theory and Action* 15: 83–97.
Foster SR (2011) Collective action and the urban commons. *Notre Dame Law Review* 87(1): 57–134.
Foster SR and Iaione C (2019) Ostrom in the city design principles and practices for the urban commons. In: Cole D, Blake H, and Rosenbloom J (eds) *Routledge Handbook of the Study of the Commons*. London: Routledge, pp. 235–255. DOI: 10.4324/9781315162782.
Hardin G (1968) The tragedy of the commons. *Science* 162(3859): 1243–1248.
Hardt M and Negri A (2009) *Commonwealth*. Cambridge, Massachusets: Harvard University Press.
Harvey D (2010) *The Enigma of Capital and the Crisis of Capitalism*. London: Profile Books.
Harvey D (2012) *Rebel Cities*. London: Verso.
Hess C and Ostrom E (2007) *Understanding Knowledge as a Commons: From Theory to Practice*. Cambridge MA: MIT Press.
Hodkinson S (2012) The new 'urban' enclosures. *City* 16(5): 500–518. DOI: 10.1080/13604813.2012.709403.
Huron A (2015) Working with strangers in saturated space: Reclaiming and maintaining the urban commons. *Antipode* 47(4): 963–979. DOI: 10.1111/anti.12141.
Huron A (2018) *Carving out the Commons: Tenant Organizing and Housing Cooperatives in*. Washington, D.C. Minneapolis, MN: University of Minnesota Press.
Iaione C and Foster SR (2022) *Co-Cities: Innovative Transitions Toward Just and Self-Sustaining Communities*. Cambridge, Massachusetts, MA: The MIT Press.
Jessop B (2015) *The State: Past, Present, Future*. Cambridge: Polity Press.
Kip M (2015) Moving beyond the City: Conceptualizing urban commons from a critical urban studies perspective. In: Kip M, Bieniok M, Dellenbaugh M, et al. (eds) *Urban Commons: Moving Beyond the State and the Market*. Basel: Birkhäuser Verlag, pp. 42–60.
Mansbridge J (2014) The role of the state in governing the commons. *Environmental Science and Policy* 36: 8–10. DOI: 10.1016/j.envsci.2013.07.006.
Marx K (1867) *Capital*, Vol. 1. New York: International Publishers, 1967.
Mattei U (2011) *Beni Comuni. Un Manifesto*. Bari: Laterza.
Merrifield A (2012) The politics of the encounter and the urbanization of the world. *City* 16(3): 269–283. DOI: 10.1080/13604813.2012.687869.
Midnight Notes Collective. (2001) The new enclosures. *The Commoner* 2: 1–15.
Miller B and Nicholls W (2013) Social movements in urban society: The city as a space of politicization. *Urban Geography* 34(4): 452–473. DOI: 10.1080/02723638.2013.786904.
Olson M (1971) *The Logic of Collective Action; Public Goods and the Theory of Groups*. Cambridge MA: Harvard University Press.
Ostrom E (1990) *Governing the Commons*. Cambridge: Cambridge University Press.
Ostrom V, Tiebout CM and Warren R (1961) The organization of government in metropolitan areas: A theoretical inquiry. *The American Political Science Review* 5(4): 831–842.

Pera M and Bianchi I (2022) Governmentality, the local state, and the commons: An analysis of civic management facilities in Barcelona. *Social Inclusion* 10(1): 115–125. DOI: 10.17645/SI.V10I1.4732.

Polanyi K (1944) *The Great Transformation. The Political and Economic Origins of Our Time*. Boston: Beacon Press.

Purcell M (2006) Urban democracy and the local trap. *Urban Studies* 43(11): 1921–1941. DOI: 10.1080/00420980600897826.

Rolnik R and Hirschhorn F (2019) *Urban Warfare: Housing Under the Empire of Finance*. London: Verso.

Rossini L and Bianchi I (2020) Negotiating (re)appropriation practices amid crisis and austerity. *International Planning Studies* 25(1): 100–121. DOI: 10.1080/13563475.2019.1701424.

Russell B (2019) Beyond the local trap: New municipalism and the rise of the fearless cities. *Antipode* 51(3): 989–1010. DOI: 10.1111/anti.12520.

Stavrides S (2016) *Common Space: The City as Commons*. London: Zed Books.

Tornaghi C (2017) Urban agriculture in the food-disabling city: (Re)defining urban food justice, reimagining a politics of empowerment. *Antipode* 49(3): 781–801. DOI: 10.1111/anti.12291.

Tullio D and Micciarielli MF G (Forthcoming) Hacking 'technical' decision-making as a neo-municipalist strategy. The case of urban commons in Naples. In: Bianchi I and Russell B (eds) *Radical Municipalism: The Politics of the Common and the Democratisation of Public Services*. Bristol: Bristol University Press.

van Laerhoven F, Schoon M and Villamayor-Tomas S (2020) Celebrating the 30th anniversary of Ostrom's governing the commons: Traditions and trends in the study of the commons, revisited. *International Journal of the Commons* 14(1): 208–224. DOI: 10.5334/ijc.1030.

3 Urban Commons-Local State Assemblage Regimes in Barcelona

3.1 Introduction

This chapter serves to familiarise the reader with the political context of Barcelona. It provides a historical account of the urban commons-local state assemblage regime in the city from the beginning of the 20th century until the recent new municipal government of BComú. An urban commons-local state assemblage regime refers to the dynamic interactions between the politics of urban commons in the city and the different rationalities (supportive, co-opting, or destructive) of the local state, including any resulting policy interventions. This concept encompasses the evolving configurations of power relations between urban commons and the local state at the city level, with the objective of understanding how urban commons and the local state come together under specific assemblage arrangements. It serves to illuminate the complex and often contradictory ways in which urban commons initiatives and the local government have interacted over time, revealing patterns of collaboration, conflict, and transformation in Barcelona's urban governance. By tracing this historical trajectory, the chapter provides a basis for understanding the contemporary political and social landscape that underpins the two specific case studies developed in later chapters.

The chapter is divided into three main sections. The first section examines the development of urban commons-local state assemblage regimes from the beginning of the 20th century, when urban commons emerged in Barcelona in the shape of a cooperative workers' movement that was supported by local governments. It also considers the Franco regime, which aimed to destroy them, and the democratic period that followed Franco's death, when urban commons re-emerged despite the initially more state-centred approach of the social democratic local government, gaining more strength later on as a response to neoliberal policies and their effects on the urban environment. Secondly, it pays specific attention to three periods: the aftermath of the 2007–2008 financial crisis, when many urban commons emerged in Barcelona as a political outcome of the anti-austerity mobilisations; the subsequent four years of conservative municipal government that, while adopting a co-opting

DOI: 10.4324/9781003398493-3

approach, developed policy interventions that supported some urban commons; and the subsequent arrival of the New Municipalist BComú government. Thirdly, it outlines the transformative agenda of BComú, which, on the one hand, developed policy interventions that strengthened the responsibility of the state in terms of local welfare and, on the other, developed policy interventions aimed at supporting urban commons, at least in principle.

3.2 Urban commons-local state assemblage regimes: from the early 20th century to the 2000s

Barcelona has a long history of revolutionary action and progressive thought, characterised by a strong tradition of self-management. In the early 20th century, this environment fostered the emergence of urban commons, particularly through the cooperative movement, supported by the rationalities and policy interventions of local governments. During the Industrial Revolution, the city emerged as one of the most significant industrial centres of the Iberian Peninsula, fostering a robust labour movement characterised by an anarchist component directly inspired by Bakunin and Fanelli (McNeill, 1999). This anarchist influence was integral in shaping the city's political landscape, fostering a culture of resistance among the working class. The movement's emphasis on direct action, workers' self-management, and anti-authoritarianism distinguished it from other labour movements of the time. As its economic model, it embraced cooperativism, which flourished between 1920 and 1930, peaking during the Spanish Second Republic (1931–1939). In those years in Barcelona, cooperatives were not just seen as economic units, but as building blocks of a new, egalitarian society. They were based on principles of mutual aid, collective ownership, and democratic governance, aiming to empower workers and communities. The cooperative culture in Barcelona permeated many areas of life, from production, with agricultural and workers' cooperatives, to reproduction, with libertarian schools and the 'Ateneus Populars' (People's Athenaeums) – spaces dedicated to the education and training of the working class (Grup de Treball Desbordes de la Cultura, 2017).

During the Second Spanish Republic, the cooperative movement in Barcelona and Catalonia received considerable support from local and regional governments, especially those that were left-leaning. This support varied in intensity and type according to the political composition of the administrations in question. The Generalitat of Catalonia (Catalan regional government), when it was under the leadership of the left-wing Esquerra Republicana de Catalunya (ERC) from 1931 to 1934, took significant steps to support the cooperative movement. The most important of these was the enactment of the 1934 Catalan Law on Cooperatives (Pérez Baró, 1989). This legislation provided a comprehensive legal framework for cooperatives, legitimising their status and operations within the economic landscape. The law was particularly notable for its progressive nature, reflecting ERC's commitment to social and economic reform. As soon as the law was adopted, the Generalitat created a dedicated Cooperative Service. This body was designed to promote and support cooperative initiatives by providing administrative assistance, legal advice, and educational programme. The creation of this service demonstrated the government's proactive approach to promoting the cooperative sector as part of its broader social and economic agenda.

At the municipal level, Barcelona City Council, which was also dominated by left-wing parties during most of the Republican period, often provided tangible support to cooperative projects. This support frequently took the form of land leases or the provision of facilities for cooperative initiatives (Museu d'Història de Barcelona, 2013). This practical support was crucial for the existence of ambitious projects, such as housing cooperatives, and large-scale initiatives, such as 'La Ciutat de Repòs i de Vacances' (The City of Rest and Holidays). It is important to note, however, that this supportive attitude was not constant throughout the Republican period. The political landscape was volatile, with shifts in power affecting policy approaches. For example, following the events of October 1934, when the Generalitat clashed with the central government, there was a period of conservative rule in Catalonia. During this period, the support given to cooperatives was less enthusiastic, although the legal framework established by the 1934 law remained in place.

Barcelona's anarcho-cooperativist culture continued throughout the Spanish Civil War (1936–1939). During these years, the city, which was an outpost of the Republican front and one of the last places to fall, saw the struggle coordinated by the CNT – 'Confederación Nacional del Trabajo' (National Confederation of Labour) – and the FAI – 'Federación Anarquista Ibérica' (Iberian Anarchist Federation). These organisations were instrumental in leading the city through a relatively long experience of collectivisation and socialisation of industries and services, with the CNT and FAI taking over factories, transport and services. Workers managed these industries themselves through democratic assemblies, abolishing hierarchical structures and seeking to create an egalitarian society. Many militants and members of the International Brigades came to Barcelona to support the Republican cause and were fascinated by the city's experiment. Among them was George Orwell, who in his book *Homage to Catalonia* (Orwell, 1938) gives one of the most vivid descriptions of Barcelona when he arrived in December 1936 as a militant of the POUM – 'Partido Obrero de Unificación Marxista' (Marxist Unification Workers' Party), an anti-Stalinist and anti-authoritarian party:

> It was the first time that I had ever been in a town where the working class was in the saddle. Practically every building of any size had been seized by the workers and was draped with red flags or with the red and black flag of the Anarchists; every wall was scrawled with the hammer and sickle and with the initials of the revolutionary parties; almost every church had

> been gutted and its images burnt. Churches here and there were being systematically demolished by gangs of workmen. Every shop and cafe had an inscription saying that it had been collectivised; even the bootblacks had been collectivised, and their boxes painted red and black.
>
> (Orwell, 1938, p. 15)

Orwell's account captures the radical social changes and the spirit of egalitarianism that permeated Barcelona during this period. The city streets were filled with revolutionary fervour, with ordinary citizens participating in the creation of what they hoped was a new social order.

This period of collectivisation and socialisation was not to last long. Franco's troops won the Civil War and imposed an authoritarian regime which lasted until Franco's death in 1975. Repression under Franco was severe: political parties were banned, the labour movement and its anarcho-cooperativist culture were weakened, and socialist intellectuals and activists were monitored, harassed and often imprisoned (McNeill, 1999). However, the subversive spirit of Barcelona did not disappear altogether. Although the regime confiscated the collectivised goods of the Civil War and ordered the dissolution of all cooperatives formed during that period, several labour and agricultural cooperatives continued to exist under the strict control of the regime's institution, the Obra Sindical de Cooperación (Cooperation Trade Union). Although heavily regulated, these cooperatives managed to maintain some degree of being controlled by their workers and solidarity between workers, ensuring that the cooperative ethos survived, albeit in a diminished way.

Furthermore, although the new laws prohibited any form of association that had not been established by the regime, many clandestine collective organisations were born in the 1950s and 1960s, including cultural centres, trade unions, and associations (Grup de Treball Desbordes de la Cultura, 2017). These underground networks were crucial for keeping the spirit of resistance alive. Cultural centres, often disguised as social clubs or religious gatherings, provided a space for intellectual exchange and the preservation of Catalan culture and identity, which was suppressed under Franco. Trade unions operated clandestinely, running great risks to organise strikes and protests. Associations, whether focused on local issues, women's rights or youth engagement, played an important role in building a sense of community and collective resilience against an oppressive regime.

Gradually, the Franco regime softened somewhat and allowed some limited and extremely controlled forms of social self-organisation. The approval of the 'Ley de Asociaciones' (Law of Associations) in 1964 legalised some forms of association that supported civil society in the anti-Franco struggle, not only in Barcelona but throughout Spain. This law was an important milestone, as it allowed the formal creation of different types of associations. Among these newly legalised associations were the 'Asociaciones de Vecinos' (neighbourhood associations), which played a crucial role in the anti-Franco movement (Andreu, 2014). These neighbourhood associations became central to organising protests and mobilising citizens against the regime (Nel·lo, 2015). Although they often focused on local issues such as housing, public services, and infrastructure, which were key concerns in the rapidly urbanising cities of Spain, especially in Barcelona, they represented a broad coalition of society, including workers, the middle class, and professionals, united by a common desire for democratic reform and social justice. The cross-class alliance within these associations was key to their strength and effectiveness. By bringing together different social groups, they were able to build a broad-based neighbourhood movement that transcended traditional class divisions. This inclusiveness was essential in creating a united front against the Franco regime and made their protests and campaigns more effective.

The democratic turn (the first municipal elections in Barcelona were held in 1979) marked a significant transition. The city, shaped by its anarcho-cooperativist tradition and the neighbourhood movement, came under the governance of left-wing forces led by the Socialist Party of Catalonia (PSC). This would continue until 2011, with the popular mayor Pasqual Maragall serving for 15 years. The initial socialist victory fostered a close relationship between organised civil society and local public institutions, as many members of the neighbourhood movement took on positions in the institutions. This integration into institutional roles led to a gradual weakening of the movement (Nel·lo, 2015). In this context, the local government rolled out the first phase of the so-called 'Barcelona Model'.[1] This model was initially characterised by social and urban policies with a strong redistributive approach, aimed to address the deficits left by the decades of dictatorship and with a will to incorporate the demands of the neighbourhood movement. The goal was to create a more inclusive and equitable city, reflecting the socialist principles that many of the new leaders espoused. However, this period was also marked by a severe economic crisis. The global recession of the late 1970s and early 1980s, coupled with rising unemployment rates, created significant challenges for the newly elected government. The public institutions were still in their infancy, and the public administration had very limited capacity to respond effectively to the widespread economic difficulties being suffered (Blanco, 2009). In response to these challenges, the local government, under the leadership of Maragall, sought to strengthen the local public institutions and lead Barcelona towards economic success. One of the most significant strategies was the decision to bid for and ultimately host the 1992 Olympic Games.

In this way, from the moment Barcelona was nominated as host city for the 1992 Olympic Games (in 1982), two distinct processes were put in motion. On the one hand, counter to the tendency of other European states, democratic political institutions and the welfare state were strengthened. The local government began to intervene in areas such as personal services and planning, supported by the regional government, which began to intervene in sectors such as education and health (Nel·lo, 2015). The intention was to create a more equitable urban environment, reflecting the socialist ideals that had gained traction in the post-Franco era. This growing role of the regional and local state apparatus produced benefits in redistributive terms. These benefits included expanding the stock of public housing, improving transportation networks, and enhancing healthcare and educational facilities. However, these state interventions were detrimental to social autonomy and to the emergence of urban commons. Local public institutions were constituted according to the 'classic public structure' based on hierarchy and bureaucracy, and produced 'classic public policy' based on a universalist but homogenising approach that left very little space for the self-managing and self-organising demands that were coming from the neighbourhood movement (Gomà and Blanco, 2016).

On the other hand, in line with the general trend in Europe, there was a rapid adoption of the neoliberal project and principles. In Barcelona, this led to a neoliberalisation of the 'Barcelona Model' characterised by entrepreneurial city management based on real estate speculation (Moreno and Vázquez Montalbán, 1991) and hosting major events, of which the Olympic Games (1992) represents only the most important of a long series (which include the 'Forum of Cultures', which was held in 2004); in addition, global companies were courted and mass tourism was encouraged. This neoliberalisation of the 'Barcelona Model' can be observed to have happened in several phases (Blanco, 2009). However, the change to this model was in fact gradual, and it can be seen that from the Olympic nomination (1986) up to the 2007–2008 crisis, the arrival of private capital and its profit-making objectives were fostered with no real regulation in place. The aggressive nature of the new model was especially evident in the real estate sector. In this context, the cooperativist tradition began to be rebuilt and new cooperatives emerged. However, although they were supported by the Catalan Cooperative Law of 1983, which built on the legacy of the 1934 Law, they always remained marginal.

In this period, a progressive separation took place in Barcelona between the local public institutions and civil society, which did not remain silent in the face of the neoliberal turn. Initially, the neoliberalised version of the Barcelona Model was not highly contested and benefited from a relatively broad consensus. However, as the years went by and the effects of this model began to have a negative impact on Barcelona's citizens, things changed, mainly thanks to the emergence of new collective actors. In fact, as the neighbourhood movement began to lose its importance in the scenario of social mobilisations, new autonomous movements emerged (Nel·lo, 2015).

Firstly, from 1985, after activists from Barcelona had gone to experience antagonistic environments in Italy, Germany, and the Netherlands, and thanks to the wide availability of abandoned spaces in the city (Piazza and Martínez Lopez, 2017), the squatting movement underwent a surge, with the emergence of several self-managed social centres. This movement produced autonomous cultural and social spaces through occupations and at the same time challenged local government policies, especially in the field of urban development. These centres became hubs for alternative cultural and political activities, fostering a sense of community and resistance against the commercialisation and gentrification of urban spaces. Secondly, new organisations that were connected to the ecologist and alter-globalist movements appeared. These had environmental claims linked to the area, such as urban and infrastructural projects and energy and consumption policies (Nel·lo, 2015). These organisations addressed issues such as sustainable urban planning, mounting opposition to environmentally destructive projects, and promoting renewable energy sources. They often collaborated with international networks, bringing global environmental concerns into the local context.

Thirdly, movements that were specifically against the neoliberal slant of the 'Barcelona Model' multiplied. Since the real estate sector was poorly regulated and speculation was rife, some of the most visible movements emerged in relation to the question of housing. The 'V de Vivienda' (H as in Housing) platform, which led the demonstration 'No tendrás casa en la puta vida' (You'll never have a house in your whole fucking life), established the housing question as a central issue in mobilisations in the city and in Spain in general (Martínez Moreno, 2018). These protests highlighted the soaring costs of housing and the displacement of long-term residents due to gentrification and speculation. However, it was only with the onset of the financial crisis that this combination of antagonistic organisations rose to gain a predominant role in the social and political space.

3.3 Urban commons-local state assemblage regimes: the 2007–2008 financial crisis, urban movements, and the rise of BComú

Barcelona was hit hard by the 2007–2008 financial crisis, although the impact was somewhat less severe than experienced in Catalonia and Spain as a whole (Davies and Blanco, 2017). This economic upheaval, which had its origins in the collapse of the United States housing market, and that subsequently swept the world, brought about profound and far-reaching economic and social ramifications for Spain. The Spanish economy, which had for years been disproportionately reliant on the construction and real estate sectors, found itself in a position of acute vulnerability when faced with this economic downturn, leading to skyrocketing unemployment rates. The housing market was hit particularly hard; property values plummeted, and mortgage defaults surged, resulting in widespread foreclosures and evictions. From 2008 to 2014, approximately 684,385 evictions were registered in Spain, with a significant proportion occurring in Barcelona (Colau and Alemany, 2014). In response, social movements such the PAH (Plataforma de Afectados por las Hipotecas – Platform for People Affected by Mortgages) emerged in 2009, fighting against evictions and advocating for housing rights, highlighting the urgent need for more equitable housing policies in the wake of the economic collapse.

At the electoral level, the crisis led to a major political shift in Barcelona, resulting in the victory in 2011 of a conservative party, Convergència i Unió (Convergence and Union – CiU from now on), after over 30 years of municipal governance by left-wing coalitions. The new government, led by Mayor Xavier Trias, fully aligned itself with the urban austerity policies that had been recommended by the European Union and taken up by the central government, which had enacted new fiscal measures and imposed stringent spending controls on municipal budgets. These urban austerity measures justified further neoliberalisation of the 'Barcelona Model'. This response to the recession involved an increased focus on privatisation and the commodification of the city's heritage and public services (Davies and Blanco, 2017). Examples of these austerity-driven policies include the implementation of a new municipal bylaw that privatised public spaces by increasing the outdoor spaces of bars and restaurants, lifting the ban on building licenses for new hotels in the historic city centre, and privatising some municipal public services such as nursery schools (Blanco, 2015).

The effects of the crisis sparked forceful social protests throughout Spain, including Barcelona. In 2011, the '15M' movement (named after the day it began, the 15th of May) erupted. This movement unfolded in 57 cities across Spain, and one of the largest concentrations of protesters gathered in Barcelona's Plaça Catalunya. This 'urban uprising' was made up of several resistance movements (Martínez López, 2016), reflecting a diverse coalition of activists, students, unemployed people, and people dissatisfied and frustrated with the established economic and social order. The movement also intersected with and amplified existing campaigns in cities, particularly regarding housing rights and the PAH, that thus gained visibility and support. The movement's encampments and assemblies in public squares became spaces for political education and mobilisation, drawing diverse participants from across society. By and large, the 15M movement called for an end to austerity measures, greater political transparency and the establishment of a more participatory democracy. While the encampments were eventually broken up by authorities (in Barcelona, this occurred on 27 May 2011, leading to significant clashes with police), the movement's impact continued to be felt in the years that followed, leading to a series of political outcomes.

This unprecedented form of urban mobilisation led to two distinct yet interconnected developments: a socio-community pathway and a political-institutional trajectory. These parallel outcomes represented the evolution and diversification of the movement's energy and ideals into more concrete and sustained forms of social and political engagement within the urban fabric of Barcelona. On the one hand, a multifaceted array of autonomous social practices – urban commons – experienced a significant surge in number and became more consolidated within the city's landscape. This ecosystem of urban commons encompassed a wide spectrum of activities and organisations, including but not limited to: sustainable energy cooperatives, which sought to democratise and decarbonise the city's energy supply; anti-eviction movements, which continued to fight against the ongoing housing crisis; community gardens, which promoted local food production and community cohesion; time banks and food banks, which facilitated resource sharing and mutual aid among citizens; workers' cooperatives, which explored alternative models of economic organisation; citizen telecommunications networks, which aimed to provide community-controlled internet access; and self-managed cultural and social centres, which created spaces for alternative cultural production and social interaction. In a research project on social innovation in Catalunya, Cruz et al. (2017) identified more than 700 urban commons. While not all of these practices had emerged alongside the 15M movement, their numbers increased significantly from the second decade of the 2000s, with the 15M serving as a catalyst (Varvarousis et al., 2020).

To address the unprecedented wave of mobilisations generated by the 15M movement and the proliferation of urban commons, the conservative government in charge of Barcelona City Council, led by CiU, adopted a relatively tolerant stance towards some of these initiatives, while continuing to pursue its neoliberal austerity agenda. The government's strategy was twofold. Firstly, it aimed to reduce visible unrest and large-scale demonstrations by giving some material concessions to the social movements and urban commons. Specifically, the CiU government focused on accommodating urban commons that were perceived as less politically threatening. This involved providing spaces and limited economic resources to certain initiatives. For example, they allowed groups to use vacant lots for community gardens or offered unused municipal buildings for social and cultural activities. However, this support was often conditional and limited in scope, designed to prevent these initiatives from evolving into more radical or politically challenging forms. To operationalise this strategy, the CiU government introduced specific policies for urban commons, including the Pla Buits (Vacant Spaces Plan) and the formalisation of a Civic Management framework, which we will examine in more detail in the following chapter. Secondly, this approach allowed the CiU administration to focus on implementing its core neoliberal and austerity-based agenda. By selectively engaging with certain urban commons, the government sought to create a façade of responsiveness to citizen demands while simultaneously pursuing policies of privatisation, budget cuts, and market-oriented urban development. This twofold approach exemplified the CiU council's attempt to navigate the tensions between grassroots demands and its own neoliberal agenda, ultimately aiming to maintain political stability while advancing their core policy objectives (Bianchi, 2022a).

On the other hand, the 15M movement triggered the rise of new left-wing political platforms, both at the national level (Podemos), and at the local level (Candidacies of Change). This political transformation represented a significant shift in the Spanish political landscape, channelling the energy and demands of the 15M movement into formal political structures. At the national level, Podemos (meaning 'We Can' in Spanish) was founded in January 2014 by Pablo Iglesias, along with other academics and activists. Podemos quickly gained traction, leveraging social media and grassroots organising techniques to build support. In the May 2014 elections to the European Parliament, just four months after it was formed, Podemos secured five seats with 7.98% of the national vote, a remarkable achievement for such a new party. Podemos continued its ascent in Spanish politics, entering the national parliament in the December 2015 general election. The party secured 69 seats in the Congress of Deputies (lower house) with 20.66% of the vote, becoming the third-largest party in Spain. This result shattered the traditional two-party system that had dominated Spanish politics since the transition to democracy in the late 1970s. In the years that followed, Podemos played a crucial role in reshaping Spain's political dynamics, eventually entering government as part of a coalition in 2020–2023. However, internal divisions and shifting political landscapes have since challenged its influence, reflecting the broader evolution of the left in Spain and signalling a turning point in the 15M mobilisation cycle.

At the local level, Candidacies of Change emerged as a singular political phenomenon in various Spanish cities, representing a new form of municipal politics that sought to translate the participatory ethos of the 15M movement into concrete local governance practices (Eizaguirre et al., 2017). These platforms were characterised by their strong emphasis on feminist, eco-socialist, and egalitarian ideals, which were not just rhetorical commitments but integral to their organisational structure and policy priorities (Thompson, 2020). Another defining feature was their close relationship with the city's social movements, whose activists were actively involved in the candidacy and played a key role in shaping their political agenda, governance approach, and legitimacy (Bianchi, 2023). This close connection is why they are referred to as 'movement parties' in the literature (Della Porta et al., 2017). In Barcelona, this movement party took form as 'Guanyem Barcelona' (Let's Win Barcelona), officially launched online on 15 June 2014, followed by a well-attended event in the Raval neighbourhood on June 26. It was launched by Ada Colau, a prominent activist widely recognised for her work with the anti-eviction platform, PAH. Colau was joined by other notable figures including Jaume Asens, a human rights lawyer, and Joan Subirats, a professor of political science. Guanyem Barcelona deliberately positioned itself as a citizen platform rather than a traditional political party.

The organisation of Guanyem Barcelona introduced several innovative approaches in its formation and operational strategies. One of the most notable was the implementation of open primaries, a democratic process where any resident of the city could participate in selecting the candidates for the municipal election. Moreover, the platform adopted a rigorous ethical code that set clear standards for its elected officials. This code included salary caps and mandated full transparency in decision-making processes, promoting accountability and integrity within the political structure. Another significant innovation was the participatory approach to defining its programme. Rather than confining policy formulation to a small group of experts or leaders, Guanyem Barcelona engaged with the public through a series of open assemblies and online consultations. This method allowed citizens to contribute to the electoral programme directly, ensuring that the policies that were proposed actually reflected the community's needs and aspirations. In addition, the platform established local groups in each of Barcelona's neighbourhoods. These groups were designed to foster grassroots participation, giving residents a direct voice in addressing local issues and ensuring that the broader political movement remained closely connected to the specific needs of each area (Eizaguirre et al., 2017).

In early 2015, due to legal issues with registering the name 'Guanyem', the platform changed its name to 'Barcelona en Comú' (Barcelona in Common – hereafter BComú). This name change did not affect the fundamental principles or organisation of the movement. BComú built a broad coalition, bringing together various left-wing and green parties, including among others Initiative for Catalonia-Greens (ICV), Podemos Barcelona, Procés Constituent, and Equo. This coalition strategy allowed the platform to unite various progressive forces in the city under a common banner. In the May 2015 municipal elections, BComú emerged as the party with most seats in the city council, winning 11 out of 41 seats with 25.21% of the vote. Although BComú was still short of an absolute majority, this result allowed Ada Colau to become Mayor of Barcelona, marking a historic shift in the city's governance (Blanco et al., 2020). The success of BComú was mirrored in other Spanish cities, where similar platforms won control of municipal governments. These included Ahora Madrid in Madrid, Zaragoza en Común in Zaragoza, and Por Cádiz Sí Se Puede in Cádiz, among others. Collectively, these victories were often referred to as the 'New Municipalist movement', representing a new approach to local governance that uses the local scale as an entry point to challenge neoliberal and austerity policies (Russell, 2019). The case of Barcelona, compared to most other New Municipalist cities in Spain, differed in that BComú managed to govern for two terms (2015–2023), giving them more time to develop and implement their left-wing political agenda.

During these two terms, however, challenging neoliberal and austerity policies was not easy. Following the electoral success of BComú in 2015 and 2019, the movement party faced numerous political challenges that tested its ability to govern effectively and maintain its transformative agenda. Operating as a minority government required constant negotiation and compromise with other parties, often diluting BComú's more radical proposals. The movement party's inexperience in institutional politics occasionally led to strategic missteps and difficulties navigating complex bureaucratic processes (Blanco et al., 2020). BComú also faced significant opposition from established political and economic elites who viewed its agenda as a threat to the established order. This opposition manifested in various forms of 'lawfare', with legal challenges being launched to thwart key policies such as housing and tourism regulations. Media attacks, often from conservative outlets, persistently portrayed BComú's leadership as incompetent or ideologically extreme, undermining public trust in its governance. Internal tensions within the coalition also emerged over time, as the pragmatic demands of governing sometimes clashed with the movement party's grassroots ideals. This led to disillusionment among some activists and supporters who felt that BComú was not pursuing radical change aggressively enough (Russell, 2019).

In addition, BComú faced opposition from higher levels of government, particularly the Catalan regional government and the Spanish national government, which at times actively worked to undermine or block municipal initiatives. The complex political landscape surrounding Catalan independence[2] further complicated BComú's position as they attempted to navigate this contentious issue, demonstrating a more mediating approach while maintaining a focus on their municipal agenda (Blanco et al., 2020). This complex set of political challenges, combined with the strain of eight years in power, contributed to BComú's electoral defeat in 2023, with the PSC taking on leadership of the city once again. This transition marked the end of the New Municipalist experiment, leaving behind a complex legacy of achievements. Indeed, during its two terms, despite numerous political challenges, BComú succeeded in implementing a transformative urban agenda that not only strengthened municipal welfare but also adopted a supportive rationality to urban commons through specific policy interventions, referred to as 'commons-sympathetic policies' (Bianchi et al., 2022).

3.4 The urban commons-local state assemblage regime under BComú: urban welfare and commons-sympathetic policies

BComú's policy priorities illustrate a novel approach to municipalism that deliberately departs from traditional state-centred models of social change. It is an approach based on a dual strategy that carefully balances two key objectives: strengthening the capacities and responsibilities of the local state, while at the same time empowering and strengthening the autonomy of civil society organisations (Bianchi, 2022b). This delicate balance is what distinguishes BComú's brand of New Municipalism from conventional or previous models – such as municipal socialism – which often place the state at the centre of social transformation efforts. Municipal socialism was a political practice with its roots in the late 19th and early 20th centuries that emphasised the role of local government in providing public services and improving living conditions. It focused on the municipalisation of key services such as water, gas, electricity, and public transport, as well as the provision of basic welfare services, such as public housing and health care (Stromquist, 2023). However, BComú went beyond mere municipalisation, recognising both the limits of state action and the importance of citizen participation and autonomy. Key to the development of these policy ideas was the concept of the commons.

BComú, like many other New Municipalist practices, extensively employed the concept of 'commons' or, more precisely, the idea of the 'common' in its discourse and political practice (Bianchi, 2023). In these cases, the concept often appears in its singular form to represent a broader paradigm of social transformation based on the idea of self-government. In this vision, self-government should permeate various spheres of society, from labour to the economy, including public institutions (Dardot and Laval, 2015). Creating self-governed public institutions means establishing bodies in which the state is not the sole decisionmaker, but where this power is genuinely redistributed and shared with civil society (Bianchi, 2024). This means creating radically democratised institutional configurations in which participation becomes embedded within the institutions themselves.

In the context of public service management, this embedded participation implies the creation of public services where members of the community are allowed to self-produce and self-distribute these services, backed by substantial financial support from the local state – for example, when public housing is provided through cooperative housing projects. Similarly, this necessitates the implementation of innovative forms of co-ownership between public and civic partners, demonstrating the potential of a hybrid provision of services, such as when energy infrastructures are co-owned by citizen cooperatives and municipalities. Likewise, this entails instances where the local state provides and distributes public services in-house, but with decision-making processes shared with civil society, such as through public utility companies with participatory governance structures (Bianchi and Russell, 2026).

In terms of policy-making, this dual approach undertaken by BComú - reinforcing the local state's role while empowering civil society's autonomy - involved different policy interventions. On the one hand, the BComú agenda placed a strong emphasis on reinforcing the responsibilities of the local state and enhancing local welfare provision through a series of state-centred policy interventions. These initiatives spanned multiple sectors, reflecting BComú's commitment to integrated social welfare that sought to address the city's contemporary challenges, emerging from years of implementing the neoliberal version of the Barcelona Model.

In this regard, one of the foundational elements of BComú's policy agenda involved the remunicipalisation of public services, with a particular focus on the management of water and energy resources. Although its efforts to bring water management back under municipal control did not come to fruition, BComú was more successful with the creation of Barcelona Energia. This was established in 2018 as a public electricity distributor with the primary objectives of promoting renewable energy use, combating energy poverty, and providing citizens with a more transparent and democratically accountable energy service. By 2021, this municipal energy company had achieved remarkable progress, providing 100% renewable energy to all municipal buildings and public lighting, as well as to over 3,000 households (Angel, 2021). The success of Barcelona Energia has not been without its challenges. The company has had to navigate complex regulatory environments and compete with established private sector players. Additionally, there have been debates regarding the appropriate scale of the company's operations and its relationship with the broader energy market. Despite these challenges, Barcelona Energia has emerged as a novel model, demonstrating the potential for municipal governments to play a more active role in energy provision, and challenging the dominant paradigm of privatised energy markets.

Housing was also a key policy area for BComú. There was a long-standing shortage of public housing in the city. Central to BComú's housing strategy was a dramatic increase in the construction of new public housing units. Between 2015 and 2019, the city initiated the construction of 4,600 new public housing units, marking a substantial increase from the 1,470 units built in the previous term (Blanco et al., 2020). This fourfold increase in building new housing showcases BComú's commitment to direct public intervention in the housing market, which was a stark departure from the more market-oriented approaches of previous administrations. In addition to new construction, BComú pursued an innovative strategy of acquiring existing properties to rapidly expand the public housing stock. Between 2015 and 2019, the city acquired 750 flats from banks and private owners, which were subsequently converted into social housing. This approach allows for a more rapid expansion of the public housing stock compared to new construction alone, while also potentially addressing issues of vacant properties in the city. As a result of these combined efforts, Barcelona's public housing stock increased from 7,000 units in 2015 to 9,500 in 2019 (Blanco et al., 2020). This represents a significant 35.7% increase over a four-year period, highlighting the scale and ambition of BComú's housing strategies. However, it is crucial to note that despite this progress, public housing still constitutes only 1.5% of the city's total housing stock (Blanco et al., 2020). This figure underscores the enormous challenge faced by BComú in transforming Barcelona's housing market, which has been shaped by decades of speculative development and underinvestment in social housing.

In relation to the tourism sector, BComú's approach represented a significant departure from the growth-oriented policies of previous administrations. The implementation of the Special Urban Plan for Tourist Accommodation (PEUAT) in 2017 stands as a cornerstone of this new approach, embodying BComú's vision for a more socially responsible tourism sector (Ajuntament de Barcelona, n.d.). The PEUAT divided the city into four zones, each with its specific regulations regarding the growth of tourist accommodation. It froze the number of tourist beds in the city centre and aimed to reduce them by 20% over time. The plan also restricted new licenses for tourist apartments in certain areas of the city and encouraged the development of tourist accommodation in peripheral areas to reduce pressure on the city centre. The implementation of the PEUAT has been a complex and contentious process. The plan faced legal challenges from the hotel industry and property owners, who argued that it infringed on their property rights and economic interests. Despite these challenges, the plan was largely upheld by the courts and has begun to show some impact on the city's tourism landscape. Early assessments indicate a slowdown in the growth of tourist accommodation in the city centre, a shift in hotel development towards peripheral areas, and a reduction in the number of unlicensed tourist apartments (Ajuntament de Barcelona, n.d.).

Beyond these more state-centred and welfare-oriented policy interventions – which are far from exhaustive – BComú also developed interventions inspired by the paradigm of the common, aimed at strengthening the autonomy and capacity of social organisations through what have been defined as commons-sympathetic policies (Bianchi et al., 2022).

One example of these commons-sympathetic policies is the Pla d'Impuls de l'Economia Social i Solidària (Plan for Promoting the Social and Solidarity Economy), which was launched in 2015 (Ajuntament de Barcelona, 2016). This ambitious programme marks a clear departure from conventional economic development strategies and has a focus on prioritising social value and cooperative principles over traditional profit-driven models. The plan, with a budget of €24 million allocated over four years, includes an unprecedented level of investment in the social and solidarity economy (SSE) in terms of the city's recent history. It employs several strategies and programmes to help the sector thrive. Central to the plan is financial support provided through grants and subsidies for both new and existing SSE ventures; this addresses the significant problems faced by these projects in accessing capital and enables them to grow. Recognising that many SSE organisations may lack business management skills, the plan also includes training programmes and assistance to help them enhance their operational capabilities (Ajuntament de Barcelona, 2016). The plan also seeks to raise public awareness about the principles and practices of the SSE, aiming to shift consumer behaviour and attract more participants to the sector. Lastly, it promotes networking and collaboration among those involved in these ventures, recognising the importance of inter-organisational cooperation in creating a resilient SSE sector. However, the implementation of this plan has not been without its challenges. While the SSE sector has seen impressive growth, it still represents a relatively small fraction of Barcelona's overall economy. Additionally, there are ongoing concerns about the long-term sustainability of SSE enterprises, particularly regarding their ability to compete within a market-driven economy without continued public support. Despite these challenges, the plan remains a significant step towards reimagining urban economic development through the spread of urban commons initiatives that drive the social and solidarity economy.

In the housing sector, BComú has also championed commons-sympathetic policies to address the city's housing crisis, with one notable initiative being the promotion of housing cooperatives through the 'Co-housing' programme

(Ferreri and Vidal, 2022). This programme represents a departure from traditional state-owned public housing policies and embraces community-led solutions and alternative models of tenure. Central to BComú's cohousing programme is a kind of 'social lease' model, known in Catalan as 'cessió d'ús'. This model, inspired by the Danish 'andel' system and similar approaches in Uruguay, offers a hybrid form of tenure that sits between renting and owning. Under this model, the municipality retains ownership of the land, and typically grants a long-term lease (often 75 years) to a housing cooperative. The cooperative then constructs and manages the housing, with members gaining the right to use a dwelling indefinitely in exchange for an initial contribution and monthly fees. By 2021, the programme had reached a modest but significant milestone: seven plots of municipal land had been transferred to housing cooperatives on long-term leases, providing homes for approximately 300 people, with additional plots already being transformed (Cabré and Andrés, 2018). However, there are challenges in scaling up this model. These include the limited availability of suitable land, complex financing arrangements, and the need for specialised knowledge among both municipal officials and cooperative members. Despite these challenges, BComú's co-housing programme represents another step towards diversifying Barcelona's housing provision through support for urban commons housing initiatives.

Beyond social and solidarity economy initiatives and housing, BComú also implemented policies that extended commons principles to other areas of social provision, such as care. One notable example is the Vila Veïna initiative. This initiative, launched by Barcelona City Council in 2021, represents an innovative approach to care, where care is conceived as a shared community task, not something private or individual. This programme aims to create a network of 'neighbourhood villages', each serving anything between 10,000 and 30,000 residents within a 250-metre radius (Keller-Garganté and Colom, 2025). The initiative establishes community hubs that generate projects and activities in close contact with the local residents. These schemes aim to improve the well-being of both carers and of those who require care, throughout their lives, but especially concentrating on two stages: early childhood and old age. By 2023, a pilot programme had been implemented in 16 areas across Barcelona, with plans for expansion city-wide. Vila Veïna emphasises community participation, encouraging residents to co-create solutions to local challenges. It also aims to make care work more visible and valued within neighbourhoods. The programme integrates various municipal services, including health, social services and urban planning, to create a more holistic approach to community care (Keller-Garganté and Colom, 2025). While Vila Veïna does not directly support the development of urban commons that provide care, it nonetheless represents an important step towards integrating a more community-oriented approach to care, both for those who provide it and for those who receive it.

This list of commons-sympathetic policies is not exhaustive and will be supplemented in later chapters by descriptions of two other key policies: the Citizen Assets Programme and the Waste-Picking Cooperative. However, it illustrates BComú's supportive rationality towards the urban commons, which was reflected in policy initiatives that aimed, at least in principle, to promote social autonomy in the urban fabric of the city.

3.5 Conclusion

In conclusion, this chapter has traced the evolution of urban commons-local state assemblage regimes in Barcelona from the early 20th century to the present day. This historical trajectory has determined the particular nature of the Barcelona case, marked by its anarcho-cooperativist culture, its tradition of self-management, and its resilience against authoritarianism and neoliberal pressures. This political tradition has profoundly shaped the evolution of urban commons-local state assemblage regimes within the city. Self-managing and progressive values are so deeply engrained in the city's political fabric that they enabled the survival and resurgence of urban commons even under adverse state rationalities and policy interventions, such as during the Franco regime, when clandestine collective organisations persisted, and in the neoliberal turns of social democratic government in the 1990s and early 2000s, when autonomous movements, including the squatting movement, environmental initiatives, and housing rights groups, rose up to challenge the negative impacts of neoliberal measures.

However, urban commons initiatives really skyrocketed after the 2007–2008 financial crisis, both as a response to the crisis and as a result of anti-austerity mobilisations. This surge was helped by a conservative government that, while adopting a co-opting rationality, selectively implemented policy interventions that made material concessions to less politically threatening initiatives. These were later actively supported by the New Municipalist government of BComú, which introduced commons-sympathetic policies aimed, albeit in principle, at promoting somewhat more autonomous urban commons. It is within this context of the explosion of urban commons and supportive policy interventions, shaped by different local state rationalities and significant political shifts in local power, that the urban commons cases analysed in the following two chapters were developed.

Notes

1 The Barcelona Model is an urban development and governance strategy that emerged in the 1980s and 1990s, focusing on the revitalisation of public spaces, extensive infrastructure improvements and the promotion of civic participation, with the aim of transforming the city.

2 The Catalan independence movement seeks the separation of Catalonia from Spain. Its recent past is marked by a controversial referendum in 2017, and there are ongoing political and social tensions between Catalonia and the Spanish government. In this context of political polarisation between those for independence and against it, BComú's approach has been one of mediation, not openly supporting independence but advocating people's right to vote.

References

Ajuntament de Barcelona. (n.d.) *Pla d'Allotjaments Turístics*. Available at: https://ajuntament.barcelona.cat/pla-allotjaments-turistics/en (Accessed: [21 December 2024]).

Ajuntament de Barcelona. (2016) Pla d'Impuls de l'Economia Social i Solidària. Barcelona.

Andreu M (2014) El Moviment Ciutadà i La Transició a Barcelona: La FAVB (1972-1986). Universitat de Barcelona.

Angel J (2021) New municipalism and the state: Remunicipalising energy in Barcelona, from Prosaics to process. *Antipode* 53(2): 524–545. DOI: 10.1111/anti.12687.

Bianchi I (2022a) The local state's repertoires of governance strategies for the urban commons: Nuancing current perspectives. *Environment and Planning C: Politics and Space* 40(8): 1784–1800. DOI: 10.1177/23996544221108333.

Bianchi I (2022b) Empowering policies for grassroots welfare initiatives: Blending social innovation and commons theory. *European Urban and Regional Studies* 30(2): 107–120. DOI: 10.1177/09697764221129532.

Bianchi I (2023) The commonification of the public under new municipalism: Commons – State institutions in Naples and Barcelona. *Urban Studies* 60(11): 2116–2132. DOI: 10.1177/00420980221101460.

Bianchi I (2024) The democratising capacity of new municipalism: Beyond direct democracy in public–common partnerships. *Policy & Politics* (published online ahead of print 2024). DOI: 10.1332/03055736Y2024D000000033.

Bianchi I, Pera M, Calvet-Mir L, et al. (2022) Urban commons and the local state: Co-production between enhancement and co-optation. *Territory, Politics, Governance* 12(9): 1333–1352. DOI: 10.1080/21622671.2022.2108491.

Bianchi I and Russell B (2026) *Radical Municipalism: The Politics of the Common and the Democratisation of Public Services*. Bristol: Bristol University Press.

Blanco I (2009) Does a 'Barcelona Model' really exist? Periods, territories and actors in the process of urban transformation. *Local Government Studies* 35(3): 355–369. DOI: 10.1080/03003930902854289.

Blanco I (2015) Between democratic network governance and neoliberalism: A regime-theoretical analysis of collaboration in Barcelona. *Cities* 44: 123–130. DOI: 10.1016/j.cities.2014.10.007.

Blanco I, Salazar Y and Bianchi I (2020) Urban governance and political change under a radical left government: The case of Barcelona. *Journal of Urban Affairs* 42(1): 18–38. DOI: 10.1080/07352166.2018.1559648.

Cabré E and Andrés A (2018) La Borda: A case study on the implementation of cooperative housing in Catalonia. *International Journal of Housing Policy* 18(3): 412–432. DOI: 10.1080/19491247.2017.1331591.

Colau A and Alemany A (2014) *Mortgaged Lives: From the Housing Bubble to the Right to Housing*. London: Journal of Aesthetics & Protest Press.

Cruz H, Martínez Moreno R and Blanco I (2017) Crisis, urban segregation and social innovation in Catalonia. *Partecipazione e Conflitto* 10(1): 221–245. DOI: 10.1285/i20356609v10i1p221.

Dardot P and Laval C (2015) *Común. Ensayo Sobre La Revolución Del Siglo XXI*. Barcelona: Gedisa.

Davies JS and Blanco I (2017) Austerity urbanism: Patterns of neo-liberalisation and resistance in six cities of Spain and the UK. *Environment and Planning A* 49(7): 1517–1536. DOI: 10.1177/0308518X17701729.

Della Porta et al. (2017) *Movement Parties Against Austerity*. Cambridge: Polity
Eizaguirre S, Pradel-Miquel M and García M (2017) Citizenship practices and democratic governance: 'Barcelona en Comú' as an urban citizenship confluence promoting a new policy agenda. *Citizenship Studies* 21(4): 425–439. DOI: 10.1080/13621025.2017.1307609.
Ferreri M and Vidal L (2022) Public-cooperative policy mechanisms for housing commons. *International Journal of Housing Policy* 22(2): 149–173. DOI: 10.1080/19491247.2021.1877888.
Gomà R and Blanco I (2016) *El Municipalismo del Bien Común*. Barcelona: Icaria Editorial.
Grup de Treball Desbordes de la Cultura (2017) *desbordar Barcelona : Un Relat Alternatiu de La Cultura a La Ciutat*. Barcelona: Pollen Edicions.
Keller-Garganté C and Colom S. (2025) Políticas locales para impulsar comunidades de cuidados: el caso de VilaVeïna. *Investigaciones Regionales – Journal of Regional Research* 61(1): 107–121. DOI: 10.38191/iirr-jorr.24.041
Martínez López M (2016) Between autonomy and hybridity: Urban struggles within the 15M movement in Spain. In: Mayer M, Thörn C, and Thörn H (eds) *Urban Uprising*. London: Pelgrave, pp. 253–278.
Martínez Moreno R (2018) *Innovación social y gobernanza multinivel. Cambio en las relaciones de poder y gestión del conflicto. Los casos de Barcelona y Madrid*. Barcelona: Universitat Autònoma de Barcelona.
McNeill D (1999) *Urban Change and the European Left: Tales from the New Barcelona*. London: Routledge.
Moreno E and Vázquez Montalbán M (1991) *Barcelona, a Dónde Vas? : Dialogos Para Otra Barcelona*. Barcelona: Ediciones de la Tempestad.
Museu d'Història de Barcelona (2013) *Cooperatives 1842-1939/BCN*. Barcelona.
Nel.lo O (2015) La Ciudad En Movimiento: Crisis Social y Respuesta Ciudadana. Madrid: Díaz & Pons.
Orwell G (1938) *Homage to Catalonia*. London: Harvest Book, 1980.
Pérez Baró A (1989) *Història de Les Cooperatives a Catalunya*. Barcelona: Editorial Critica.
Piazza G and Martínez Lopez M (2017) More than four decades of squatting: Cycles, waves and stages of autonomous urban politics in European cities. In: Martínez Lopez M (ed) *The Urban Politics of Squatters' Movements*. London: Palgrave, pp. 229–245.
Russell B (2019) Beyond the local trap: New municipalism and the rise of the fearless cities. *Antipode* 51(3): 989–1010. DOI: 10.1111/anti.12520.
Stromquist S (2023) *Claiming the City: A Global History of Workers' Fight for Municipal Socialism*. London: Verso.
Thompson M (2020) What's so new about new municipalism? *Progress in Human Geography* 45(2): 317–342. DOI: 10.1177/0309132520909480.
Varvarousis A, Asara V and Akbulut B. (2020) Commons: A social outcome of the movement of the squares. *Social Movement Studies* 20(3): 292–311. DOI: 10.1080/14742837.2020.1793753.

4 A Rhizomatic Urban Commons-Local State Assemblage

Can Batlló Sociocultural Centre and the Citizen Assets Programme

4.1 Introduction

This chapter analyses the case of the Can Batlló sociocultural centre, created by a group of neighbourhood residents and activists in Barcelona in 2011. This case is used to show how rhizomatic urban commons-local state assemblages can be formed under different political regimes, when the local state is governed by either conservative or left-wing governments. Conservative administrations, such as the one that governed Barcelona City Council from 2011 to 2015, can implement policy interventions that provide economic and legal support to some urban commons by making them material concessions. These interventions are often part of a co-opting and taming rationality adopted by conservative local governments in politically turbulent times, such as in the aftermath of the 15M movement, when the local state needs to increase its legitimacy and broaden consensus. However, they can be used strategically by urban commons to build rhizomatic urban commons-local state assemblages, in order to acquire material resources, maintain their self-governing autonomy and strengthen their political action. This shows that a co-opting and taming rationality does not necessarily generate co-opted and tamed urban commons. Even conservative governments, using this rationality, can provide a window of political opportunity for urban commons to build rhizomatic assemblages. However, it is mainly when leftist governments come to power that rhizomatic urban commons-local state assemblages can be strengthened if urban commons manage to take advantage of the implementation of commons-sympathetic policies such as those adopted by Barcelona in Common (BComú).

The chapter begins by examining the historical context that led to the creation of the Can Batlló sociocultural centre. By analysing its 35-year journey from an abandoned industrial site to a relatively successful urban commons, it shows how the group involved was able to take advantage of the political situation that existed after the financial crisis and create a rhizomatic urban commons with the conservative local government. The local government adopted a co-opting rationality as part of its urban austerity agenda, but developed

DOI: 10.4324/9781003398493-4

policy interventions that materially supported the development of this urban commons without limiting its self-governing capacity. The narrative then moves on to analyse the evolution of Can Batlló under the BComú government, highlighting the introduction of a commons-sympathetic policy, the Citizen Assets programme, which aimed to support the transfer of public assets in the city, and which granted Can Batlló an unprecedented 30-year lease. This action significantly strengthened the rhizomatic assemblage and protected the development of Can Batlló's urban commons from future adverse political turns. The chapter concludes by reflecting on the journey undertaken by Can Batlló, and what this story tells us about the possibility of building rhizomatic urban commons-local state assemblages, under both co-opting and supportive rationalities. However, the chapter also highlights that often this possibility is not available to more contentious and politically risky urban commons, since the local state, irrespective of its political colour, selectively applies rationalities and political interventions to urban commons in the city.

4.2 Building a rhizomatic urban commons-local state assemblage: neighbourhood struggles, the neoliberalisation of urban development, and the financial crisis

In the case of the Can Batlló sociocultural centre, the construction of the urban commons-local state assemblage did not happen overnight and took decades, in fact almost 35 years, to come into being. The history of this assemblage is intertwined with the history of the city's urban development and of the Barcelona Model, with the neoliberal policies promoted by the Socialist Party of Catalonia's (PSC) governments and the dramatic impact of the crisis creating the political opportunity for its emergence.

During the Franco regime, Barcelona's approach to urban development left significant urban deficits, especially in peripheral working-class neighbourhoods (Borja, 2009). The industrial area of La Bordeta, in the Sants-Montjuïc district, was one of them. At the end of the dictatorship, its population density was high, and it lacked many public facilities and spaces compared to the city average. However, the La Bordeta neighbourhood had an empty space that could provide a solution to this deficit. From the end of the 19th century, the Can Batlló industrial estate, a huge walled textile complex, had occupied around 14 hectares, almost 25% of the area of the neighbourhood. The factory ran until 1964, when, due to the crisis in the textile industry, it was closed down and transformed into around 700 workshops rented by workers and artisans, giving rise to the so-called 'City of Trades' (Roman and Corbella, 2014). The factory was owned by the Muñoz-Ramonet family, one of the most important entrepreneurial families in Barcelona, and known for its relationship with the pro-Franco elites.

As soon as the factory closed down, the Sants Social Centre, the main neighbourhood organisation, began to make demands for the area to be used for public facilities and spaces. These demands were in fact quite modest. As one neighbour put it, 'we made demands, but quietly' (interview), but what is true is that as far back as the 1970s, there was a social group that was already reclaiming these spaces (Soler, 2014). In response to this demand, when the General Metropolitan Plan (PGM) was approved in 1976, the entire Can Batlló site was designated as Area 17: Change of Use for Urban Renewal, i.e. an 'urban area that includes land with inadequate buildings or uses, but capable of absorbing deficits in roads, green spaces and facilities' (Area Metropolitana de Barcelona, 1976). The PGM Area 17 regulations allowed the existing uses to continue until the proposed conversion was approved. However, the PGM did not define the intended conversion, which was left to be detailed in a later plan. This designation was positively received by the neighbours of La Bordeta, who waited for the city council to approve the detailed plan. Yet, this plan took a long time to be negotiated and, in the end, was not drawn up in the way the neighbours had expected.

From the democratic turn, during the development of the first phase of the 'Barcelona Model' under the socialist governments led by the PSC (1980–1986), the city council's approach to urban development was to compensate for urban deficits through small-scale projects which would provide both the suburbs and central areas with public facilities and spaces. In this first phase of the model, the city council did not draft any detailed plans and did not implement public facilities and spaces on the Can Batlló site, as there were neighbourhoods in even greater need than La Bordeta. Subsequently, the pre-Olympic period (1986–1992) was marked by unprecedented urban development in Barcelona to prepare the city for the big event: several public spaces were regenerated, new public facilities were constructed, and important infrastructural changes were made. However, even during this period, the Can Batlló site was not redeveloped due to a lack of interest on the part of the city council, which did not consider the Can Batlló site to be a priority area for transformation, probably because of its peripheral location and because, as one activist commented, 'it was an area linked to the needs of the neighbourhood and not to the needs of the city's Olympic ecosystem' (interview). The opportunity to transform the area did not arise until the 2000s, with the transformation of the adjacent main road, the Gran Via de les Corts Catalanes.

As the main thoroughfare from the airport to the city, Gran Via became the subject of a major regeneration project, with 2 km of the road being put underground, a new railway station being constructed and the development of 'Europa Plaza', a 34-hectare area business district. However, it was at this time that the 'Barcelona Model' began its neoliberal transformation and began to welcome private interests to take part in public regeneration projects. In this way, the transformation of the Gran Via aroused the interest of property owners who were aware of the process and understood the possibilities of profiting from real estate speculation. In fact, the entire Can Batlló site was owned by 'Gaudir', a property company created by the Muñoz-Ramonet family to take advantage of the general growth in the construction sector.

Despite the initial qualification made in the PGM, in 2002, after several negotiations with the city council, Gaudir managed to obtain approval for a detailed plan that included a significant allocation for residential use (57,000 square metres), with a portion designated for social housing (25%–50%) and the remainder for housing sold at market prices. However, this was not enough for Gaudir, which had greater ambitions in terms of profits. Following further negotiations with the city council, involving the Sants Social Centre defending its demands, the final modification of the plan in 2006 resulted in a higher allocation for residential use (116,427 square metres), with a majority for housing sold at market prices and smaller portions for affordable (12%) and social housing (20%). Of course, none of the Sants Social Centre members was completely satisfied with the result of these negotiations, but they understood that they had no alternative but to accept the owner's conditions. In the end, in the words of one of the neighbours, 'we got something too, we obtained the approval of a detailed plan, with a green area and with the realisation of some of the public facilities that we had requested' (interview). The development had to be carried out through a 'compensation system',[1] which required Gaudir to carry out the entire redevelopment, including the public part, under the control of the public administration. In other words, with the approval of the 2006 amendment, Gaudir, now Immogaudir, obtained the right to dedicate 18,000 square metres of the Can Batlló site to private development, privatising land that had previously been designated as public (Bianchi, 2018).

Although Immogaudir already had a final design from an architectural firm, the redevelopment never got off the ground. A year after the approval of the detailed plan in 2006, the 2007–2008 housing crisis hit. Immogaudir, realising that apartments that were initially going to be sold at 6,000 euros per square metre would sell for much less or would very probably not be sold at all, did not proceed with the project and postponed it indefinitely. The residents of La Bordeta continued to make demands that the Can Batlló site should be for the neighbourhood and kept up their pressure on the city council, which responded repeatedly that the redevelopment project would begin shortly. However, despite the promises made by the city council, in the end they understood that, in the words of one resident, 'with the crisis, not one brick will be laid' (interview). In other words, with the onset of the crisis, the residents of La Bordeta became aware that the wait for the public facilities and spaces that had been promised to them seemed futile, since the 14 hectares of the Can Batlló industrial site were destined to remain an unused and inaccessible area. They decided to turn this threat into an opportunity and intervene so that these public spaces and facilities would be created.

In 2009, the neighbours of La Bordeta created the 'Can Batlló és pel barri' platform (Can Batlló is for the Neighbourhood) – (CB platform), supported by the Sants Social Centre and soon joined by many activists from the urban mobilisations that anticipated the 15M movement (Soler, 2014). As one activist said:

> It wasn't important who did it, the owner or the city council, the important thing was to open up the space to the neighbourhood.
>
> (Interview)

To do this, they launched a countdown campaign, dubbed 'Tick-Tock'. This consisted of setting a specific date, 11 June 2011, just after the date of the local elections (the elections were to be held on 22 May, with the new government to take power on 11 June). They threatened to occupy the factory if the project had not been started by that date. Despite pressure on the city council and weekly Tick-Tock demonstrations, the situation did not seem to be reaching any kind of resolution. Over this period, it appeared more and more likely that the factory would be squatted. Moreover, during the meetings of the CB platform, a discourse emerged among its members. The discourse was:

> What's lacking in our neighbourhood? Whatever facilities the city council does not provide us with, we can provide ourselves.
>
> (Interview)

In other words, during the Tick-Tock campaign, which put the possibility on the table of the site being squatted, there was an important shift in the demands of the platform: for some, the demand for public facilities and spaces became a demand for self-management.

The threat of the site being squatted was not well received by either of the other actors – the city council and Immogaudir – due to the turbulent political and social scenario that was in place (Sánchez Belando, 2017). In May, the 15M protests broke out, and Plaça Catalunya became the scene of anti-austerity protests and was repeatedly occupied. The owners of the site began to fear that this could also happen in Can Batlló and asked the city council to protect the industrial estate with a police presence on the day of the threatened occupation. However, the left-wing government, which was still in power, did not want to damage its reputation in the days before the elections and confirmed that no police forces would be sent. In the end, the conservative party, Convergència i Unió (CiU), won the elections on 22 May, but was only set to take power on 11 June. This meant that the PSC no longer cared about the day of the occupation, and the new government, although it did care, could do nothing to stop it. In other words, no political force was going to intervene. This pushed the owners to negotiate. After all, Immogaudir had nothing to lose: its right to build on part of the land had already been ratified in the 2006 PGM amendment, and the rest of the land would have to be handed over to the city council after the redevelopment in any case.

On 6 June, Immogaudir's lawyer called the Sants Social Centre and told its members that they were willing to give them one of the warehouses. This proposal, although tempting, was rejected by the CB platform because they were not asking Immogaudir for a building, but for Immogaudir's building to be given to the city council, which would then give it to the CB platform. The logic of the CB platform, in addition to its demands to self-manage the public facilities and spaces, was to ensure that the space would be definitively released from private ownership and be allocated to the community in La Bordeta. This could only be achieved by making the warehouse public property. In this way, the CB platform openly challenged the city council's approach to urban development. The left-wing administrations had sold public land to encourage private speculation, and the CB platform sought to recover it, using the public nature of the property as a guarantee. As one neighbour said:

> Although we want to govern ourselves, we want to defend what is public and we want to preserve public heritage, land and buildings, not like the city council did for so many years.
>
> (Interview)

With this logic in mind, negotiations were initiated, with the participation of Immogaudir, the left-wing city council in its last days in power, and the CB platform. On 9 June, it was agreed that the 1500 square metre 'Bloc 11' warehouse would be transferred to Barcelona City Council, which in turn would give it to the CB platform to use.

The choice of Bloc 11 was due to the fact that it was already defined as a public facility in the detailed plan, that it was a listed building, and that it was close to the main entrance of the industrial estate (Marcé, 2014). The city council signed a contract with the platform (in fact, with the Sants Social Centre, since the CB platform was not a legal entity) which established a temporary lease for allowing Bloc 11 to be used by the CB platform; this was a contract that had to be renewed every year. Some voices within the platform stressed that this agreement was a limited achievement compared to the possibility of reclaiming the whole plot. However, the majority of those involved realised that this was an offer that would be impossible to improve upon. If they had occupied the space, they would never have been able to defend it for long and would most likely have been evicted in the end, going back to where they had started. In this way, the CB platform was granted the use of a large warehouse, and on 12 June 2011, armed with the keys, they triumphantly entered the Can Batlló site. They reopened a space that had been closed to the public for more than 35 years, and began self-managing it.

In other words, in the case of Can Batlló sociocultural centre, the long and complex journey of forming the urban commons-local state assemblage highlights the intricate interplay between a particular city council formation, its evolving urban development policies, and community activism in Barcelona. The neoliberal turn of the Barcelona Model, driven by socialist governments led by the PSC, added to the dramatic impact of financial crises, fostered the political conditions necessary for the emergence of this unique assemblage, which, we argue, took on a rhizomatic form.

4.3 Practicing a rhizomatic urban commons-local state assemblage: the Can Batlló sociocultural centre under the conservative government

After the triumphal entry into the building and the ensuing celebrations, the first general assemblies of the Can Batlló sociocultural centre were convened. First of all, members of the assembly tried to clarify what functions the building should have. Priority was given to facilities that the neighbourhood lacked, and it was decided to create a library, an auditorium, and a meeting room with a café on the ground floor, and a sports room and several activity rooms on the first floor. In order to create, manage, and coordinate these spaces, various independent commissions and working groups were formed, including ones dubbed Activities, Library, Space and Design, Communication, Negotiation, Maintenance, and Infrastructure and Management Model. These groups always reported what they were doing to the General Assembly, which was the supreme governance body, operating according to the principle of deliberative democracy (Marcé, 2014). Gradually, the spaces and activities of Bloc 11 took shape. In September 2012, after about a year of work, the 'Josep Pons' library, meeting room, auditorium, and café were inaugurated to coincide with the annual neighbourhood festival. At the same time, a cultural programme, with an avowedly critical, albeit apolitical, perspective, was organised, which included film projections, workshops, reading clubs, and exhibitions. All this was strictly open to everyone and free of charge. Thus, after about a year of collective work, Bloc 11 became a self-managed sociocultural centre offering alternative and non-standard sociocultural services governed according to the principles of horizontal and direct democracy (Parés et al., 2017).

During this initial period, the General Assembly also carried out some deep internal reflection on the type of self-management it wanted to develop. In November 2012, the 'Bloc 11 Internal Regulation' document was published. In this document, the assembly defined the nature of the sociocultural centre in the following way:

> (Bloc 11 sociocultural centre) is a neighbourhood space that is self-managed by the 'Can Batlló for the Neighbourhood' platform, in the form of direct democracy. This space, located in the Can Batlló industrial site, is municipal property, but it has been transferred to the community of Sants

and La Bordeta. It is therefore not a municipal facility, but a public facility, of the neighbourhood and for the neighbourhood.

(Plataforma Can Batlló és pel Barri, 2012)

This new emphasis on the public nature of the space does not mean that the issue of self-management lost its importance. In several parts of the document, the preservation of self-government appears as a key feature of the project:

All processes (decision-making, participation, information, etc.) will be decided autonomously by the General Assembly, commissions or working groups, without external interference.

(Plataforma Can Batlló és pel Barri, 2012)

The document also states:

(Bloc 11 sociocultural centre) must move towards economic self-sufficiency at all levels of its organisation (…) and possible funding should not jeopardise the independence of Bloc 11.

(Plataforma Can Batlló és pel Barri, 2012)

In other words, it was very important that Bloc 11 maintained both its self-governing and material autonomy. However, despite these claims, and the efforts made to be economically self-sufficient with money raised by the café and by organising other activities and events (Plataforma Can Batlló és pel Barri, 2015), in reality the Sants district of the city council (which was the governmental level responsible for negotiating with the CB platform) played an important role in the development of the Bloc 11 sociocultural centre. Under the political guidance of the CiU government, the district supported Bloc 11 with financial and infrastructural contributions and also helped by adopting a special approach to legal and administrative procedures. On the grounds that it was investing in its 'real estate assets', the Sants district carried out all the necessary building work to guarantee the building's structural safety, paid all the bills, such as water and electricity, provided workers through a programme run by the city council to reintegrate unemployed people, and paid the cost of other building work that had not originally been foreseen but could be considered structural, such as the soundproofing of the auditorium. The city council did not have a fixed annual budget for these contributions but modified them according to the needs of sociocultural centre, which were discussed in regular meetings with the Sants district. In the first year, the district spent 120,000 euros on the infrastructure of the Bloc 11 sociocultural centre, while in the following years, the contribution was set at around 20,000/30,000 euros (Plataforma Can Batlló és pel Barri, 2015).

In addition, according to the neighbourhood residents interviewed, the Sants district adopted an approach that was very flexible. This approach allowed the project to come to life despite the limitations imposed by a bureaucratised and standardised administration; the approach distinguished and valued those requirements that were truly necessary from those that were merely formal legal requirements. For example, in the case of health and safety regulations, the Sants district was strict about the library's fire regulations because of the flammable material there, but was more flexible about the café's licences. As the manager of the Sants district himself mentioned:

> at Can Batlló we always had to skirt the limits… I'm not saying that we did not follow the rules, but if we had followed the rules strictly, we wouldn't have got anywhere.
>
> (Interview)

All these issues were discussed and negotiated during the fortnightly meetings between the CB platform and the district, in which a constructive relationship of mutual trust was gradually built up. This constructive relationship was described by the activists as one of 'friction' and by the public administration as one of 'coexistence'. According to the activists, the friction was due to the fact that:

> our management model and their management model are different, because the administration has rules to follow, a structure to make work, which by definition goes against the empowerment and self-management of the people, but we do not reject the relationship.
>
> (Interview)

According to the city council, this coexistence was due to the fact that:

> Can Batlló is not outside the institutions as such, but it has codes that are considered a new form of institutionality. It is not antagonistic – it does not live in a situation of confrontation with the state and public administrations – but coexists with a series of formulas, unwritten but practised, of dialogue with the administration.
>
> (Interview)

Regardless of the point of view of each actor, it can be said that the success of the Bloc 11 sociocultural centre was the result of the ability of the CB platform's members to combine an exemplary model of self-management in terms of democratic quality with the promotion of the public character of the cultural centre. But it was also due to the constructive relationship they were able to establish with the Sants district and the city council, overcoming the aggressive antagonism of some squatted social centres and the arguably too-friendly collaboration of some civil society and third sector organisations. In this way, they developed a model that allowed them to participate in productive discussions and to receive material support from the city council, even from a right-wing one, while maintaining their self-governing capacity. This model, which combined decision-making independence with public support, was not seen as a contradiction by the CB platform members. In the words of one of the activists:

> what they (the city council) do is to invest in their assets, and what we do is use them and manage them as public facilities for the neighbourhood. Use and management mean that we decide on our cultural programme, the activities and our economic model.
>
> (Interview)

This statement highlights the peculiar rhizomatic nature of the urban commons-local state assemblage in the case of Can Batlló sociocultural centre. On the one hand, it acknowledges the material support that the city council provides to the centre, while on the other hand, it emphasises the capacity of the centre to maintain its decision-making independence in terms of its day-to-day management. Given its success in developing such a politically beneficial assemblage, the CB platform decided to extend this approach beyond the construction of the sociocultural centre to other areas and activities as well.

Under the same conservative government, the CB platform gradually asked for more space to expand its project, a request that was granted. Different activities were set up in the new spaces, which were always allocated through temporary contracts. Some short-term activities (such as workshops or reading groups) were held in additional spaces in the Bloc 11 sociocultural centre. Other activities were complementary to the Bloc 11 sociocultural centre, and were set up permanently in their allocated spaces, such as a carpentry workshop, a community kitchen, a documentation centre for social movements, a mobility workshop, a collective print works, a family space and urban gardens. This inclusion of other temporary and permanent activities transformed the project. The initiative expanded from just self-managing the Bloc 11 sociocultural centre into a larger self-management project, that we call the 'Can Batlló project', which included several activities, of which the sociocultural centre was only one. All the activities were selected by the General Assembly and had to operate according to the principles of the social and solidarity economy and generate social or economic return (or both) for the Can Batlló project. In particular, in the case of permanent activities, they had to also be approved by a joint committee made up of representatives of the CB platform and the city council district, with the aim of avoiding the creation of for-profit activities and promoting individual economic gain (Plataforma Can Batlló és pel Barri, 2012).

Subsequently, and still under the CiU government, the Can Batlló project continued to expand, launching three large, long-term projects to demonstrate that community management could also be an alternative to public management in other sectors (Parés et al., 2017). These projects were presented to the city council for approval. The first was 'La Borda', a housing cooperative that aimed to build more than 40 apartments on a public site through a 75-year public land lease to the cooperative; the second was 'Coopolis', an agency that aimed to promote the social and solidarity economy at the city level and also to address the high unemployment rate in the district; the third was 'Arcadia', a cooperative school that aimed to provide primary and secondary education. Only 'La Borda' was approved by the CiU government, while the other projects had to wait for the change of government that happened in 2015, when BComú won the elections. The schemes remained the same, the property or land remained in public ownership and was temporarily and autonomously allocated to each project. However, they formed part of the larger Can Batlló project. They therefore provided a social and/or economic return to Can Batlló and participated in its General Assembly, giving shape to a successful management model that worked through a network of commissions and autonomous projects, each managed horizontally according to a rationale of democratic cooperation (Parés et al., 2017).

At first glance, the CiU government's approach of providing support to the Can Batlló project might seem peculiar. However, as explained in the previous chapter, this support was part of a specific rationality deployed by the local government that was aimed at taming the wave of self-management practices that were spreading across Barcelona in the aftermath of the 15M movement. To achieve this, the government, in addition to accommodating requests for material support that it received from certain self-managing practices that were not seen as particularly politically risky, adopted several concrete policies, including the Urban Voids Plan and Civic Management Framework. The Urban Voids Plan was implemented in 2012 with the following aim: 'to stimulate the use of unused land in the city of Barcelona, through activities of public interest of a temporary nature, led by public or non-profit entities, encouraging the involvement of civil society in the regeneration of the urban fabric of the city'(Ajuntament de Barcelona, 2013). Vacant plots were temporary assigned through public calls to community organisations, and the city council assumed the costs of upgrading the plots and supplying electricity, water, etc., while the remaining expenses had to be met by the organisation itself.

The Civic Management Framework aimed to regularise the various forms of self-management of the city council's public cultural facilities, such as its Civic Centres, Youth Centres, and Neighbourhood Centres. While some of these public facilities were directly managed by the city council and some were outsourced to private companies, others were managed by community organisations under the Civic Management model.[2] However, this management model was underdeveloped from the legal and financial point of view and did not provide sufficient stability. Under the new framework, approved in 2015, Civic Management is defined as 'an instrument of citizen participation through which a non-profit organisation can manage facilities and municipal services that are subject to indirect management with the aim, among others, of promoting citizen participation in public interest initiatives, including its management' (Ajuntament de Barcelona, 2015). The management of the facilities is temporarily assigned to a non-profit organisation which receives a fixed annual contribution from the city council that, if it is insufficient for covering costs, can be complemented by external funds. This framework, despite improving the legal and financial stability of the Civic Management facilities, had a series of limitations that would only be (partially) addressed when BComú came to power.

Through these two programmes, the CiU government tried to institutionalise the more 'moderate' self-managing practices, while retaining some degree of control over them: the assignment of spaces in the Urban Voids Plan was carried out in a very limited space of time, and the cultural production in spaces under Civic Management remained under the supervision of the city council. Meanwhile, the CiU government adopted a much harsher stance towards more politically radical or autonomous spaces, as evidenced by several high-profile eviction cases. For instance, in 2014, the attempted eviction of those squatting the Can Vies sociocultural centre highlighted the government's lack of tolerance for spaces that posed a greater political challenge. The eviction led to widespread protests and riots. Similarly, the eviction of La Carboneria in the Sant Antoni neighbourhood in 2014 demonstrated the administration's willingness to use force to dismantle spaces that did not conform to their vision of 'acceptable' sociocultural centres.

These actions reveal a clear pattern: spaces that maintained a strong anti-institutional stance or engaged in more radical political activities were targeted for dismantlement, while those willing to operate within the boundaries set by the local government were more likely to be tolerated or even incorporated into official programmes. This selective approach underscored the CiU government's strategy of controlling certain forms of self-managing practices by providing formalised public support, as in the case of Urban Voids and Civic Management facilities, or by providing non-formalised public support, as in the case of the Bloc 11 sociocultural centre, while suppressing others, effectively drawing a line between what it considered acceptable forms of self-managing practices and what it viewed as unacceptable. In addition, by supporting the more institutionalised cases, the city council was promoting its urban austerity agenda, by shifting the cost of social reproduction onto local communities. The cost of both formal and informal support for these self-managed facilities and spaces was lower than the cost of publicly provided ones (Bianchi, 2022b).

In sum, the CiU government's rationality, embedded within an agenda of austerity urbanism, was a calculated strategy to institutionalise and control more moderate forms of urban commons while suppressing more radical elements (Bianchi, 2022b). Policy interventions such as the Urban Voids Plan and the Civic Management Framework provided avenues for collaboration with less politically risky initiatives. Within these governmental rationality and policy interventions, the Can Batlló sociocultural centre showed a remarkable ability to take advantage of a politically volatile situation in the wake of the 15M movement in order to create a rhizomatic assemblage. In fact, Can Batlló sociocultural centre has established a solid relationship of trust with the city council and has benefited from institutional financial and infrastructural support. In this way, it has been able to expand its activities and spaces, promoting a robust model of community management without compromising its core values (Bianchi, 2022a). In other words, it has managed to maintain its self-governing capacity while receiving material support from the local government. This delicate assemblage, achieved through strategic negotiation, pragmatic cooperation and an unwavering commitment to the principles of self-government, was further consolidated when the BComú platform came to power.

4.4 Consolidating a rhizomatic urban commons-local state assemblage: the Can Batlló project and the Citizen Assets programme under the BComú governments

The election of BComú to the city government in 2015 marked a significant positive shift in the relationship between the CB platform and the city council. This improvement was partly due to the close ties and occasional overlap between CB platform participants and BComú members, with some of the activists now coming to hold positions within public institutions. However, to maintain its principles of independence from public institutions, the Can Batlló assembly made a crucial decision: those who became part of the municipal government could no longer officially participate in the Can Batlló project. The enhanced relationship was primarily driven by BComú embracing the 'commons' discourse as a central tenet of their political agenda (Bianchi, 2023). As mentioned in the previous chapter, this new administration aimed to provide greater autonomy to social collectives in Barcelona and viewed the Can Batlló project as both a tangible manifestation of their political philosophy and a powerful symbol of it. Consequently, the new government offered full support to the Can Batlló project, taking several significant steps forward.

The city council approved a revised plan for the entire site, officially recognising the CB platform as a key stakeholder (Ajuntament de Barcelona, 2017b). It also committed to providing 65 million euros of the 150 million needed for adapting the buildings of the Can Batlló site to become public spaces and facilities, in line with its expansive fiscal agenda. Moreover, while maintaining the overall distribution of private and public use areas and the number of square metres reserved for housing to be sold at market prices, the new plan introduced important qualitative modifications. Buildings that had been allocated to the CB platform but had previously been scheduled for demolition were now earmarked to be preserved, recognising their historical and cultural value. The plan incorporated projects that had previously been demanded by the CB platform but had not been incorporated during the CiU government, such as Coopolis (which was focused on the social and solidarity economy) and Arcadia (a cooperative school), expanding the scope of the entire Can Batlló project. The new administration also showed itself willing to maintain the relationship of trust built up during their previous term in office, with regular meetings taking place between the CB platform and city officials which facilitated ongoing communication and problem-solving.

Furthermore, and most importantly, the city council began to develop a comprehensive legal framework to formalise and standardise the transfer of urban spaces and facilities – as Civic Management facilities – to social collectives. This intention to create a commons-sympathetic policy culminated in the creation of the Citizen Assets programme. Launched in 2017 following an extensive participatory process involving members of self-managed sociocultural facilities and spaces (Bianchi, 2024), this programme aimed to establish a theoretical and normative foundation for transferring both public facilities and spaces to non-profit community organisations. The Citizen Assets programme merged the existing Civic Management Framework with public space transfer initiatives such as the Urban Void plan into a single, cohesive scheme. It introduced a novel conceptualisation of facilities and spaces as 'assets', framing them within the context of urban commons. They were defined as 'locally-embedded institutions of collective action that produce public goods and services not managed by the state' (Ajuntament de Barcelona, 2017a). This innovative approach led to the establishment of a new set of administrative rules, procedures, and governing bodies designed to facilitate and support the transfer of these assets to non-profit community organisations.

The Citizen Assets programme introduced several key innovations to streamline the process of transferring public assets to community organisations. Firstly, it established the Citizen Assets Board, a centralised municipal body made up of officers from various departments. This board coordinates asset transfers and contract renewals, consolidating decision-making power that had previously been dispersed throughout the various city districts. Secondly, the programme implemented a new set of criteria for awarding or renewing transfers. These criteria reflect the social vocation of non-profit community organisations, emphasising participation and internal democracy, local community engagement, social impact and return, as well as environmental stewardship. Thirdly, the Citizen Assets Catalogue was created as a comprehensive, publicly accessible census of all public assets transferred to non-profit community organisations. Fourthly, the programme introduced the Community Balance report, a self-assessment tool so that the organisations that manage these assets can evaluate their own performance. Fifthly, the Citizen Assets Office was established, providing dedicated public officers to support community organisations throughout the asset management process, from preparing applications to evaluation. Lastly, the programme is overseen by a Participatory Governance Space, enabling citizen actors to monitor the implementation and effectiveness of the programme. In essence, the Citizen Assets programme represents a significant administrative reform, centralising and codifying the transfer of public assets in Barcelona. It overhauls existing administrative processes, rules, and bodies, creating a comprehensive policy framework that unifies and enhances various pre-existing programmes (Bianchi, 2024).

The Citizen Assets programme marked a significant milestone for the Can Batlló project, offering it a path to consolidate its position and overcome some longstanding challenges. The project had become an emblematic example of the type of social autonomy that the BComú local government sought to promote citywide through the Citizen Assets scheme. Recognising this, the city council decided to provide substantial empowering support to the Can Batlló project. In a ground-breaking move, the city council revised the agreement concerning the transferred assets, bringing it under the new Citizen Assets programme. Through a resolution passed in the Barcelona municipal plenary,[3] the council granted use of the spaces to the Can Batlló project for an unprecedented 30-year period, with the possibility of a 20-year extension (Ajuntament de Barcelona, 2019). Initially, this extension was met with mixed reactions within the Can Batlló project. Some members viewed it as making their relationship with the city council excessively formal, potentially compromising the independence they cherished. They feared that such a long-term commitment might lead to increased institutional control or diluting the project's grassroots nature. However, after internal discussions and debates, the members who recognised the benefits of this extended agreement managed to persuade those who were initially resistant. They argued that the long-term security offered by this arrangement might allow for more ambitious planning and sustainable development of the project. As one activist who supported the extension explained:

> We didn't want to sign it (the agreement extension) just because we have some kind of obsession with the law; it was more for the feeling of saying: we can take advantage of the fact that there is a friendly government to generate something that could last longer in the future.
>
> (Interview)

In this way, it was recognised by the Can Batlló members that the city council could provide considerable stability to the Can Batlló project, but without tying this support to any specific administrative requirements, beyond the need to keep the space public and open to everyone. In this way, the Can Batlló project has the freedom to plan its activities in the long term, without fearing that the local government might revoke its management in subsequent election cycles. The BComú government justified this decision by underlining the importance of the public services and facilities being offered by this self-managed space and the savings that this entailed for the municipal budget. Estimating the cost to the public administration of carrying out equivalent management, they underlined that: 'if the city council were to take on the services offered by the organisation [CB Platform], it would entail an annual municipal investment of 1.43 million euros […] while a total of 1.1 million euros of public investment has been invested in Can Batlló since 2011' (Ajuntament de Barcelona, 2019).

This statement might suggest that the BComú government adopted a co-opting rationality towards Can Batlló that was similar to that of CiU, working within a framework of austerity urbanism and shifting the cost of social reproduction onto communities. However, the decision to transfer the Can Batlló site to the CB platform for 30 years appeared to be driven not by cost-saving measures but by a genuine political commitment to enhance Can Batlló's self-management capabilities. This initiative was in line with the council's wider vision of supporting self-management practices across the city, as evidenced by the adoption of the Citizen Assets programme. Furthermore, this approach was underpinned by increased public spending, as in the case of the Can Batlló site, and an urban agenda that reaffirmed the crucial role of the local state as a provider of public services. As a result, the BComú government's support for the Can Batlló project appeared to reflect a supportive governance rationality rather than a co-opting one, despite the real savings for the municipal budget (Bianchi, 2022b).

However, this rationality was not used throughout the city or for all cases of self-managing practices. The BComú government also displayed a selective rationality. The case of the Antiga Massana, a sociocultural centre born in a squatted public building in the Raval neighbourhood in 2020, illustrates this nuanced reality. Despite the precedent set by Can Batlló's 30-year lease, the city council did not grant a similar long-term agreement to the Antiga Massana, which was demanding this type of lease. Instead, the BComú government offered this self-managed space a lease of four years that could be renewed, in line with all other self-managing practices in Barcelona. As expressed by one public officer: 'A concession like Can Batlló's has to be approved by the plenary. We need to respect the protocols for transferring public spaces' (La Vanguardia, 2023). This solution was not received well by the activists of the sociocultural centre, who adopted a highly confrontational approach with the local government, ultimately leading to no agreement being reached. This decision highlights the selective nature of local government support, even under a left-wing administration like BComú. Despite this selective rationality, however, it must be recognised that this local government maintained a commitment to keep communication open with all self-managing practices, even when they were unable to meet all their demands, such as with the Antiga Massana.

In summary, the BComú government, like the CiU government that had preceded it, adopted a selective rationality towards various self-managing practices. However, while CiU's rationality drew a clear line between practices that were institutionally acceptable, with the aim of co-opting them, and those that were to be dismantled, BComú's selective actions were framed within a context of acceptance and dialogue with all projects, but choosing to openly support some over others. In the case of the Can Batlló project, this support was particularly clear. The support provided by the BComú government significantly reinforced the rhizomatic urban commons-local state assemblage. Through the innovative policy of the Citizen Assets programme and the unprecedented 30-year lease agreement, the government created a framework that respected and enhanced the project's self-governing capacity while providing crucial institutional backing. Although this framework was not well received by many members of Can Batlló, who feared that their independence might be undermined, it actually allowed Can Batlló to maintain its grassroots character and decision-making independence, while at the same time benefiting from increased stability and resources. The capacity of those leading the Can Batlló project to overcome their reservations reveals a pragmatic approach to engaging with institutional support. By accepting this long-term commitment, Can Batlló effectively insulated itself against potential changes in the political climate, ensuring its ability to plan and operate autonomously for decades to come.

4.5 Conclusion

This chapter has explored the emergence and development of a rhizomatic urban commons-local state assemblage in Barcelona, focusing on the case of the Can Batlló sociocultural centre. The Can Batlló sociocultural centre's journey from an abandoned industrial site to a relatively successful urban commons illustrates how such assemblages can strengthen urban commons' political action under both conservative and left-wing governments, albeit through different mechanisms and with varying degrees of support that respond to different local government rationalities. The formation of this assemblage was deeply intertwined with the history of Barcelona's urban development, the neoliberal turn taken by the 'Barcelona Model', and the effects of the 2007–2008 financial crisis. These factors created a political opportunity for Can Batlló to emerge as an urban commons, driven by the tenacious activism of local residents and their ability to take advantage of the politically volatile post-15M landscape. Under the co-opting and taming rationality of the conservative government, which proposed policy interventions that made material concessions and institutionalised more moderate self-governing practices while suppressing radical elements, the Can Batlló sociocultural centre managed to establish a rhizomatic assemblage with the city council based on a relationship of 'friction'. This relationship helped the Can Batlló collective to reap the benefits of material concessions without compromising its core values regarding its independence.

The transition to the left-wing BComú government in 2015 marked a significant shift in the relationship between Can Batlló and the local state, reinforcing the rhizomatic assemblage. BComú's supportive rationality for the urban commons culminated in the development of a commons-sympathetic policy, the Citizen Assets programme, which provided a comprehensive legal framework for transferring public assets to social collectives. As part of this programme, the Can Batlló urban commons was granted a 30-year lease, ring-fencing land and economic resources for the coming years and protecting them from unfavourable electoral cycles. This occurrence shows that it can be useful for urban commons to have a friendly local government and take advantage of its policy interventions, since the benefits gleaned can extend well beyond the term of the electoral mandate. However, while both conservative and leftist governments, albeit driven by different rationalities, may adopt policy interventions that materially support urban commons, such as the Can Batlló sociocultural centre, and ultimately contribute to the construction of rhizomatic local state-urban commons assemblages, they do not follow the same procedures when dealing with more contentious and politically risky urban commons in the city. One such example is the Puigcerdà informal settlement, which we will examine in the next chapter.

Notes

1 In Spain, there are three systems of land development: the compensation system, the cooperation system, and expropriation. The difference between the cooperation and compensation systems is that while in the first case, the administration is responsible for the development on privately owned areas, in the second case, the owner is responsible for this development. In both cases, the private owner is guaranteed development rights.

2 The Civic Management Model is a management model used by Barcelona City Council to transfer the management of public facilities – cultural centres, community centres, youth clubs, etc. – to non-profit grassroots organisations.

3 The transfer of public assets in Barcelona can be granted for a maximum of four years and can then be renewed. To grant an asset for longer than this, the resolution must be approved by the municipal plenary.

References

Ajuntament de Barcelona. (2013) *Mesura de Govern Pla Buits*. Barcelona.

Ajuntament de Barcelona. (2015) *Model de bases de la gestió cívica d'equipaments, per activitats i serveis municipals de l'Ajuntament de Barcelona (procediment de pública concurrència)*. Barcelona.

Ajuntament de Barcelona. (2017a) *Bienes Comunes: Un marco para la gestión comunitaria de los bienes públicos*. Barcelona.

Ajuntament de Barcelona. (2017b) *Memòria. Modificació del Pla General Metropolità. Sector Can Batlló*. Barcelona.

Ajuntament de Barcelona. (2019) *Concesión para la gestión comunitaria y vecinal de Can Batlló | Sants-Montjuïc*. Barcelona

Area Metropolitana de Barcelona. (1976) Articulo 367 Definición - Àrea metropolitana de Barcelona. Plan General Metropolitano. Area Metropolitana de Barcelona.

Bianchi I (2018) *In, Against, Beyond and Through the State. Limits and Possibilities of Urban Commons in Barcelona*. Barcelona: Universitat Autònoma de Barcelona; Venezia: Università IUAV di Venezia.

Bianchi I (2022a) Empowering policies for grassroots welfare initiatives: Blending social innovation and commons theory. *European Urban and Regional Studies* 30(2): 107–120. DOI: 10.1177/09697764221129532.

Bianchi I (2022b) The local state's *repertoires of governance* strategies for the urban commons: Nuancing current perspectives. *Environment and Planning C: Politics and Space* 40(8): 1784–1800. DOI: 10.1177/23996544221108333.

Bianchi I (2023) The commonification of the public under new municipalism: Commons – State institutions in Naples and Barcelona. *Urban Studies* 60(11): 2116–2132. DOI: 10.1177/00420980221101460.

Bianchi I (2024) The democratising capacity of new municipalism: Beyond direct democracy in public–common partnerships. *Policy & Politics* (published online ahead of print 2024). DOI: 10.1332/03055736Y2024D000000033.

Borja J (2009) *Luces y Sombras del Urbanismo de Barcelona*. Barcelona: UOC.

La Vanguardia. (2023) *Los 'okupas' de la antigua Massana exigen su cesión por medio siglo*. Available at: https://www.lavanguardia.com/local/barcelona/20230217/8763509/ocupas-antigua-massana-exigen-cesion-medio-siglo.html (Accessed: 21 December 2024).

Marcé J (2014) Dos anys a Can Batlló: somnis que es fan realitat. In: Lacol (ed.) *Inventari de Can Batlló: Teixint Una Història Col·lectiva*. Barcelona: Riera de Magoria, pp. 95–117.

Parés M, Ospina S and Subirats J (2017) *Social Innovation and Democratic Leadership Communities and Social Change from Below*. Cheltenham: Edward Elgar Publishing.

Plataforma Can Batlló és pel Barri. (2012) *Bloc Onze: Document de Règimen Intern*. Barcelona.

Plataforma Can Batlló és pel Barri. (2015) *Memòria. Funcionament Econòmic Can Batlló*. Barcelona.

Roman D and Corbella X (2014) Jugant a reporters a la ciutat dels oficis. In: Lacol (ed.) *Inventari de Can Batlló: Teixint Una Història Col·lectiva*. Barcelona: Riera de Magoria, pp. 55–67.

Sánchez Belando MV (2017) Building alternatives to the creative turn in Barcelona: The case of the socio-cultural centre Can Batlló. *City, Culture and Society* 8: 35–42. DOI: 10.1016/j.ccs.2016.11.001.

Soler J (2014) La lluita veïnal d'una vida. In: Lacol (ed.) *Can Batlló: Teixint Una Història Col·lectiva*. Barcelona: Riera de Magoria, pp. 81–95.

5 An Arborescent Urban Commons-Local State Assemblage

The Puigcerdà Informal Settlement and the Alencop Waste-Picking Cooperative

5.1 Introduction

This chapter analyses the case of the Puigcerdà informal settlement, which emerged in Barcelona in 2011 in the aftermath of the 2007–2008 crisis and was formed by sub-Saharan immigrants. This case is used to show, first, the changing nature of urban commons-local state assemblages and, second, how arborescent assemblages can be constructed under different political regimes when the local state is governed by both left-wing and conservative governments. This is particularly true for urban commons composed of marginalised and exploited migrant communities, which can become contentious and politically risky for local governments. In terms of this type of urban commons, the chapter illustrates how conservative governments, such as the one that governed Barcelona from 2011 to 2015, adopted policy interventions as part of a co-opting rationality that initially tolerated these urban commons out of economic and political expediency, creating rhizomatic local state-urban commons assemblages. However, such assemblages rarely last long: when these urban commons become more contentious and politically risky, that is, when they begin to demand administrative, labour, and housing rights from the local state, and when they challenge existing legal frameworks and power structures, conservative governments typically dissolve these assemblages or transform them into arborescent ones. The same rationality, albeit with adaptations, is employed by leftist governments such as Barcelona en Comú (BComú), which, when they succeed conservative governments, find it difficult to make policy interventions that genuinely support contentious and politically risky urban commons, such as the Puigcerdà informal settlement. However, the experience of BComú also shows the learning capacity of left-wing local governments, which, with strong political will, can also produce commons-sympathetic policies that help to build more rhizomatic urban commons-local state assemblages, even when these involve contentious and politically risky urban commons composed of marginalised and exploited migrant communities.

The chapter begins by examining how the informal settlement of Puigcerdà, created by sub-Saharan immigrants, emerged as a rhizomatic

DOI: 10.4324/9781003398493-5

assemblage under the co-opting and taming rationalities of the conservative government. The chapter then describes how this assemblage was dismantled when it became contentious and politically risky, leading to those living there being evicted and the creation of a policy intervention, the Informal Settlement Plan, that completely deprived the community of its capacity for self-government. The narrative continues with the creation of a seemingly commons-sympathetic policy designed for sub-Saharan migrants living in the Puigcerdà urban commons: the Alencop waste-picking cooperative. This illustrates the willingness of both the conservative and BComú governments to support urban commons, but also the limitations of both governments in terms of granting these sub-Saharan migrants, and exploited and marginalised communities in general, any real capacity for self-government. The chapter then examines BComú's evolving approach, including the creation of the street vendor cooperative Diomcoop, which also targeted the sub-Saharan migrant community. This case demonstrates a potential shift towards more supportive commons-sympathetic politics, capable of building more rhizomatic urban commons-local state assemblages. The chapter concludes by reflecting on the difficulties of changing institutional practices and mindsets, even within progressive administrations, towards this type of urban commons, while acknowledging the potential for learning and improvement in the creation of more genuinely supportive commons-sympathetic policies.

5.2 Building a rhizomatic urban commons-local state assemblage: migration flows, the financial crisis, and the rise of the Puigcerdà informal settlement

In the case of the Puigcerdà informal settlement, the construction of the urban commons-local state assemblage appears to have occurred within a relatively short period of time, especially when compared to the Can Batlló sociocultural centre. However, the history of its development needs to be understood in the context of various different local government policies regarding migration flows and how the dramatic impact of the 2007–2008 financial crisis pushed these migrant communities, exposed to multiple threats of exclusion, to turn to eking out a living in the city in an informal way.

From the 1980s onwards, Southern European countries began to receive significant migration flows, particularly from Latin America and Africa, driven by the demand for cheap labour in their labour markets (Arango, 2000). In Spain, between 2002 and 2007, primarily due to the boom in the construction and agricultural sectors, the immigrant population more than doubled and made Spain the largest recipient of migrants in Europe (Domínguez-Mujica et al., 2014). In addition to migrants from Spain's former colonies, a substantial sub-Saharan population arrived in the country. These were mainly young men aged between 20 and 45, who quickly found employment in the agriculture and construction industries (Isusi and Corral, 2007). This immigrant population's living conditions have consistently been far worse than those of other immigrant groups, such as people from Spain's former colonies. This disparity is primarily due to: (i) precarious and poorly paid working conditions at the very bottom of the production chain, which force these individuals to live on the brink of subsistence; (ii) unstable and sometimes irregular administrative statuses that deny them access to citizenship rights, including the right to vote; and (iii) differences in religion and language that hinder cultural integration (Haan and Maxwell, 1998). These conditions have been perpetuated by state institutions that, despite facilitating the arrival of this collective, have never attempted to address these issues and have even exacerbated them by tightening immigration laws and not pursuing adequate workplace inspections, allowing this group to be exploited and dominated in the pursuit of competitive economic growth. However, in some cases, it is precisely the harsh living conditions imposed by market and state forces that push sub-Saharan immigrants to self-organise within the informal economy, creating alternative forms of subsistence and empowerment, as in the case of Barcelona.

During the 2007–2008 financial crisis in Barcelona, sub-Saharan immigrants who had previously been employed in the construction and agricultural sectors suddenly found themselves in a condition of multiple exclusion: shut out of both the formal labour and housing markets, and often living without documentation. The left-wing coalition had not developed policies to address this issue because, as one resident noted, 'sub-Saharan immigrants were an invisible group whose condition never entered the public debate' (interview). They were redirected to mainstream social services, but this was an ineffective strategy since these services were designed for a very different demographic profile. As a result, sub-Saharan immigrants developed survival strategies by forming informal settlements throughout the city, where they could engage in informal housing solutions and economic activities, mainly waste-picking, to cope with their condition (Pradel-Miquel, 2017).

According to a study conducted by the XAPSLL organisation, the number of informal settlements occupied by sub-Saharan immigrants in Barcelona increased from 265 to 695 between 2008 and 2011, with most of them located in the Poblenou neighbourhood – a former industrial area in Barcelona that has been characterised by a strong working-class ethos, providing refuge for marginalised groups (Sales Campos A, 2013). Nevertheless, these informal settlements never lasted very long. Since they were mainly on private property, the possibility of being evicted was always looming. When it happened, the sub-Saharan groups had to search for another place to live and they eventually occupied other vacant factories. Some of the interviewees defined this process as the sub-Saharan people's circular occupation phenomenon. It was during this circular process that the Puigcerdà informal settlement took place.

In August 2011, a group of 20–30 sub-Saharan immigrants, who had been evicted from another factory in the area, discovered a vacant factory at 127 Carrer Puigcerdà. This vast space, covering 12,000 square metres and consisting of numerous warehouses occupying two whole blocks, became their new shelter and a base for their informal economic activities, primarily waste-picking. At the time of the occupation, the factory was owned by Finca Riana S.L., a real estate company primarily owned by the Iglesia Baciana family, who were also involved in various women's empowerment projects in the Global South through their private foundation, Maite Iglesias Baciana. Although the property was earmarked for regeneration under the 22@ Plan,[1] it had never undergone redevelopment due to its location on the very edge of the neighbourhood.

Due to a combination of factors – such as the vast size of the space, its location on the outskirts of Barcelona, and the worsening conditions faced by many sub-Saharan immigrants – the Puigcerdà informal settlement grew larger very rapidly. According to one of its first inhabitants, the population grew from 20 to 30 people in the first few days to 100 after one week and 200 to 300 after one month. Although it is impossible to make a precise estimate of the number of inhabitants there, the Puigcerdà settlement grew very large, becoming, as one politician in charge described it, 'a city within the city' (interview). This growth was not only due to increasingly more people living there but also to the large number of people and companies drawn to the settlement during the day to engage in business related to the informal waste-picking economy. In fact, Puigcerdà became the main metropolitan hub for waste-picking activities, attracting more than 500–800 people every day.

Waste-picking usually encompasses all activities related to the informal handling of waste, ranging from collecting, composting, sorting, and processing to selling (Dias, 2016). In the case of Puigcerdà, waste-picking was mainly related to the collection of metal waste and technological appliances from public spaces. Legally, this activity is supposed to be performed by private waste management companies, that are in charge of the collection of metal waste that is then sold to steel or other recycling companies. As well as these waste management companies, waste collection can also be performed by individuals, who can sell waste to waste management companies or directly to recycling companies as long as there is proof of the transaction. Nevertheless, despite the purchase of waste metal from individuals being legal, the activity of individuals collecting it is not. In Barcelona, as established by the Civic Ordinance of 2005, waste-picking in public spaces is an illegal activity that can incur fines of up to 500 euros. However, it has always been somewhat tolerated by police forces. This is because it is an activity that only really takes place in the outskirts of the city and is almost invisible to the eyes of locals and tourists, and it ensures a source of income to people who have no space in the formal labour market.

Waste-picking increased sharply in the aftermath of the financial crisis in Barcelona, contributing to 22% of the volume of the waste metal industry in 2013 (Gremi Recuperaciò de Catalunya, 2013). Waste management and recycling companies particularly appreciated waste pickers' labour as they were able to achieve a level of waste sorting accuracy that was impossible to achieve through mechanised processes (Gremi Recuperació de Catalunya, 2013). However, even if a person worked all day long, making an acceptable living through waste-picking would be very hard. Per kilo, waste metal sales prices ranged from 0.6 to 0.9 euro for aluminium, to 4.5 euro for copper, and to 0.16 euro for other metals. This meant that a waste pickers' average earnings ranged between 10 and 15 euro per day (Gremi Recuperaciò de Catalunya, 2013) leaving sub-Saharan waste pickers under the poverty line.

In other words, the main economic activity of sub-Saharan immigrants – waste-picking – did not provide them with adequate self-sufficiency; instead, it was an activity that benefited the more powerful actors in the waste-picking chain. This is why it was essential for the sub-Saharan immigrants to find other forms of subsistence to complement waste-picking. Occupying the Puigcerdà factory provided a solution to this. Within the walls of Puigcerdà, the immigrants were able to create informal domestic spaces, meeting their housing needs without the burden of paying rent. They engaged in various informal economic activities there beyond waste-picking, including operating a restaurant, running a second-hand shop as well as a bicycle workshop open to Barcelona residents. They also participated in mutual support networks, pooling resources and helping one another with daily tasks to secure their livelihoods and even save money to send to their families in Africa. Although it is important not to romanticise this type of living arrangement, as it emerged from conditions of extreme poverty and exclusion, the Puigcerdà settlement represented a means by which sub-Saharan immigrants could live by employing an integrated form of subsistence. As exemplified by the following quote from one of the resident of Puigcerdà, this allowed them to live according to their values and practices, creating a space where they could maintain their dignity and cultural identity amidst exclusion and exploitation.

> This was our place. We liked the life within the factory. If they had allowed us, we would have liked to keep living there together, in our way of understanding life.
>
> (Interview)

The large number of inhabitants and the complexities of managing the informal economic activities meant that co-habitation at Puigcerdà was not easy. In this environment, there were many conflicts: over sleeping arrangements, and in terms of inter-ethnic and inter-generational rivalries and unbalanced power dynamics, where certain groups dominated others based on nationality and their position in the economy of the waste-picking chain. Thus, the make-up of the group of Puigcerdà inhabitants was highly unequal, mirroring the inequalities in the 'outside' world. Nevertheless, despite the challenges of cohabitation, the sub-Saharan inhabitants managed to establish an organisational structure to address the problems and conflicts that arose daily. They formed a number of sub-groups according to nationality, each with its own representative. These representatives were responsible for negotiating when problems and conflicts arose and served as spokespeople in negotiations with institutions and civil society organisations. While far from being a perfect or equitable system, this organisation – based on national groups, spokespeople, and weekly meetings – enabled the sub-Saharan community to organise life inside the factory and shape their future relationships with civil society organisations and institutional actors.

Initially, according to residents and activists, the Puigcerdà informal settlement was tolerated by the private owner and the city council. The private owner decided not to take legal action against the squatters, and the local government, governed by the conservative Convergència i Unió (CiU) coalition, decided to turn a blind eye to the occupation. This approach represented a convenient choice for the city council, and was rooted in a rationale of co-opting and taming. By allowing these occupations and waste-picking activities, particularly within the Puigcerdà informal settlement, the city council did not have to resolve their condition of multiple exclusion, as the immigrants were dealing with it by themselves. However, it was precisely this approach that allowed the urban commons-local state assemblage to be constructed in a rhizomatic way: within it, the sub-Saharan immigrants could develop their self-governing capacity, maintaining their aspirations and identities. This rhizomatic nature, from the perspective of the local state, did not arise thanks to the local government's participation in the material sustainability of the urban commons – which had instead constructed a way to sustain itself through informal practices – but was instead thanks to the adoption of a permissive approach to their informal status, driven by a taming and co-opting rationality. Without this approach, the assemblage might have been dismantled, because often, informal activities, such as squatting or a waste-picking economy, can be deemed illegal by the state and therefore subject to destruction, should the state choose to act (Bianchi, 2022b). And this is exactly what happened when the political conditions changed.

5.3 Dismantling a rhizomatic urban commons-local state assemblage: the eviction of the Puigcerdà informal settlement and the Informal Settlement plan under the conservative government

Barcelona City Council's approach to the Puigcerdà informal settlement shifted when several factors made it into a political risk. Firstly, the settlement spanned approximately 12,000 square metres in Poblenou. Municipal authority was non-existent in this vast area, and control of it lay entirely with the sub-Saharan inhabitants. Secondly, the factory's reputation as a marginalised space threatened the city's image, prompting many to ask questions about how this 'Third World' situation could exist in modern Barcelona. Most importantly, Puigcerdà became a place where a collective of sub-Saharan inhabitants emerged as a political force, organising to challenge their exclusion and exploitation, and achieving a potentially dangerous degree of empowerment. Since this situation increasingly threatened the 'Barcelona Model', a direct intervention carried out by the city council seemed inevitable. As one resident remarked: 'When African people are self-organised, it is not convenient for them (the city council)' (Interview). The city council understood that, to eliminate this risk, it had to evict the residents, even though this eviction would take away their means of subsistence.

The official reasons given by the city council for the eviction were different. The eviction was justified on the grounds of health and safety risks, the illegality of the waste-picking economy, and, most notably, the private ownership of the buildings.

Regarding health and safety, the city council argued that conditions were unacceptable, and action was needed. One politician stated:

> "(Within the Puigcerdà factory) the sanitation was embarrassingly bad, since there was no water, no electricity, and there was rubbish was all over the place," adding that "people were exposed to life-threatening risks because of the structural lack of safety of the building."
>
> (Interview)

These conditions were confirmed by reports commissioned by the city council to the police, the fire brigade, and the Red Cross. However, the Puigcerdà inhabitants did not perceive their situation as hazardous and repeatedly requested the city council to facilitate access to running water and electricity to improve their health and safety conditions. These requests were consistently denied on the grounds that the factory was privately owned. Moreover, the city council occasionally shut down the public fountains around the factory, further worsening their health and safety conditions. In other words, despite genuine concern from the social services department, it appeared that the city council was intentionally preventing improvements being made in order to justify the eviction.

Regarding the informal waste-picking economy, the city council consistently stigmatised the Puigcerdà informal settlement, asserting that it was a hub for shadowy and possibly illegal dealings. As one public officer remarked:

> Some people in the waste industry were doing very well. Containers from waste management and recycling companies would go there to load up before heading to the port for shipping. There were people there who made good money by taking advantage of the wretched lives of many others.
>
> (Interview)

Although the city council seemed to understand the exploitative nature and dubious aspects of this economic chain, it took no actions to address those issues and instead used the illegal nature of this activity to justify the eviction. Beyond these official reasons, the most compelling argument was that the property was privately owned. The city council maintained that because of this, nothing could be done to prevent the eviction.

At the end of 2011, the private owner initiated legal action to evict the inhabitants of the squat. The media justified this action by suggesting the owner intended to redevelop the property into a Self-Sufficient Island (La Vanguardia, 2012). The Barcelona Self-Sufficient Island was a public plan aimed at developing a new housing model based on local energy production and sustainable resource management (Ajuntament de Barcelona, 2012b). However, despite media reports suggesting the plan was already underway, it was not expected to be implemented any time soon, since the project was still in its preliminary phase. This indicates that although the development of the estate into a Self-Sufficient Island might have lent more legitimacy to the legal action, it was not as urgent as portrayed in the press.

Various sources confirmed the pressure exerted by the city council on the owner to proceed with the eviction. Firstly, in the final eviction ruling (Juzgado Primera Instancia 21, 2013), it is mentioned that due to the building's lack of structural safety, the city council would fine the owner if no legal action were taken. Secondly, one of the Puigcerdà residents, who claimed to have spoken with a member of the Iglesia Baciana family privately, stated that 'it was not the owner who pushed for the eviction, as the owner never complained' (interview). Thirdly, an activist confirmed this, saying:

> The city council put pressure on the owners because they were accountable for any accident that happened in Puigcerdà, but in reality, they did not care about this. The true will to end the occupation came from the city council itself.
>
> (Interview)

In other words, the fact that the building was privately owned facilitated the city council's intended outcome. Despite its consistent support for eviction as a solution to the occupation, the city council shifted responsibility onto the owner. While this does not absolve the owner of responsibility, it can be concluded that Finca Riana S.L. supported the city council's political will by undertaking the legal action necessary to carry out the eviction, considered the only way to dismantle the informal settlement and ultimately curtail the political action of its residents.

From the moment the first legal action was initiated, the sub-Saharan community, organised around the 'Som 300' (We are 300) movement, put together a more coordinated political action strategy to save the informal settlement from being broken up and to defend their basic rights. They quickly gained the support of various local social movements and civil society organisations, including the Poblenou Neighbourhood Association, human rights organisations, a team of lawyers, and left-wing opposition parties. Initially, they focused on fighting for three main rights: social, labour, and administrative rights. In terms of social rights, they demanded the right to use the factory as a place to live and work; they resisted eviction and called on the public administration to undertake basic improvements to the building, such as providing running water and electricity. Regarding labour rights, they sought the right to work legally as waste pickers and be formally integrated into the waste recycling sector, advocating the legalisation of waste-picking and the creation of a cooperative. In terms of administrative rights, they campaigned for formal recognition within Spanish society in the shape of residence permits.

The first significant outcome of this struggle, which was achieved with legal support, was the cancellation of the initial eviction order in March 2012 due to a formal technicality. However, despite the hopes that this generated, legal action was soon reactivated by Finca Riana S.L., and the eviction appeared inevitable. Nevertheless, the sub-Saharan political movement continued to organise marches and events, advocating not only for the factory's inhabitants but also for the rights of the entire African migrant community in Barcelona.

As the eviction date approached and the media and social pressure intensified, the city council decided to limit the damage being done to its reputation by providing subsistence to those who would be displaced by the eviction. To this end, it implemented a public programme, dubbed the 'Oficina del Pla d'Assentaments Irregulars' (OPAI, Irregular Settlements Plan), aimed at offering an integrated form of subsistence specifically for this social group. The objective of the OPAI was to 'support all people living in informal settlements in Barcelona, assisting them towards social, economic, and administrative inclusion, and guaranteeing decent living conditions in terms of housing, employment, and administrative status, with the aim of eradicating informal settlements in Barcelona' (Ajuntament de Barcelona, 2012a). The OPAI became operational in January 2013, with the Puigcerdà settlement as its first main challenge. However, despite its goal of providing subsistence, the OPAI proved more 'aesthetic than effective', consistently prioritising evictions over providing support, addressing political problems at the expense of social ones.

In the lead-up to the Puigcerdà settlement being broken up, the OPAI's primary focus was to 'skim off' as many residents as possible to limit the settlement's growth and mitigate the anticipated humanitarian crisis. Some residents joined the OPAI scheme, while others, distrusting the institutions, resisted until the eviction was imminent. By the end of 2013, over 260 sub-Saharan immigrants had been housed through the OPAI (Ayuntamiento de Barcelona, 2014), but finding sufficient accommodation in such a short time proved a logistical challenge. Initially, most residents were placed in guest houses, which incurred significant costs. A more integrated social services plan was developed, pairing individuals with social workers to create personalised work plans, but this support took time to materialise.

The OPAI also provided limited services to give advice to the inhabitants on their administrative status, as Spanish law required immigrants to hold full-time, one-year employment contracts to apply for residency permits. Despite the city council's efforts to secure exceptional permits, only four residents had received them by the end of 2013 (Ajuntament de Barcelona, 2014). Additionally, the OPAI developed a training and employment plan, subsidising companies to hire people with irregular status; however, only 20 work contracts were secured in the first year. In summary, the OPAI's efforts to provide integrated form of subsistence were largely inadequate, leaving many residents with temporary accommodation but without any means for long-term survival, as they lacked the means to find employment or regularise their administrative status, or the ability to continue their informal economic activities. As one sub-Saharan resident remarked:

> In a way, he (the politician in charge of the Social Rights Department) ensured that people weren't thrown onto the streets by putting them in hostels and paying out a lot of money, as he said. But why was this money spent? Because you can't live in a hostel … you need food, you need work. It is indeed a way to help, but it was on his terms.
>
> (Interview)

In other words, while the city council succeeded in preventing the majority of recorded residents from ending up on the streets, it ultimately worsened conditions for some, as it could not guarantee the integrated subsistence that they had somehow managed to provide for themselves within the factory.

Barcelona City Council understood that it was impossible to provide the same integrated subsistence that the sub-Saharan inhabitants had managed to achieve within the factory, yet it never questioned that the eviction order was the only solution. Despite the sub-Saharan inhabitants' requests to continue living in the Puigcerdà settlement in order to support themselves through waste-picking and to maintain the community they had created, the city council never considered that Puigcerdà could have been preserved and improved with its support. As one opposition politician remarked:

> At no point did the CiU government take a personal and human approach, nor did it empathise with the possibility that something could have been developed there (at the Puigcerdà factory) along with the sub-Saharan inhabitants.
>
> (Interview)

This is because the primary objective was not to provide for the subsistence of the sub-Saharan group, but as one neighbour put it, the aim was 'to disintegrate them, disperse them, and, if possible, make them disappear' (interview). In other words, the main objective was to eradicate the settlement and disband the sub-Saharan community, thereby weakening their self-governing capacity.

Once the eviction took place, the inhabitants would lose their ability to meet in assemblies, discuss actions and strategies, organise marches, and structure their political action.

As a result, despite all the campaigns, protests, appeals, and marches, the eviction order arrived in June 2013 and was executed on 24th July of the same year. The deployment of police forces was considerable, with 50 police vans from the regional police arriving early in the morning. After the eviction, some residents accepted the accommodation offered by the OPAI, while another group continued their struggle by moving into the nearby Sant Bernat Church for three more days before also deciding to accept the OPAI's accommodation or go their own way. Those who did not use the OPAI – whether due to distrust of institutions, exclusion from the Red Cross census, or risk of repatriation – relied on their solidarity networks and support from civil society organisations, which continued to provide assistance to all the residents.

In summary, in the case of the informal settlement of Puigcerdà, when the urban commons-local state assemblage became too contentious and politically risky for the city council – because it had allowed this marginalised and exploited migrant community to articulate its rights – the city council decided that it could no longer adopt a tolerant rationality and that the assemblage had to be dismantled and destroyed, since the dismantling and destruction of this assemblage would curtail the empowering political action of sub-Saharan immigrants (Bianchi, 2022a). However, the destruction of the assemblage through eviction was not complete; the assemblage continued in another form. The same city council, still dominated by CiU, tried to reformulate it in a different guise, in a more hierarchical and arborescent form, by creating the waste pickers' cooperative.

5.4 Rebuilding an urban commons-local state assemblage in an arborescent form: the Alencop waste-picking cooperative under the conservative and BComú governments

In 2014, the conservative city council included a pilot project for a waste-picking cooperative on its agenda. The project aimed to provide integrated support to a selected group of sub-Saharan immigrants, most of whom had previously resided in the Puigcerdà informal settlement. This support encompassed housing and administrative assistance, while the cooperative itself was designed to formalise waste-picking activities, promote cooperative values, and empower workers. The cooperative project was supported by a technical team of two people from an association called Procoop, which was part of Labcoop. Labcoop is a non-profit cooperative dedicated to promoting cooperative social entrepreneurship projects. The plan was that the project would develop in two phases, with the cooperative gradually increasing in members.

In the first phase (2014–2015), 15 individuals were selected from 35 candidates proposed by the OPAI, primarily immigrants from the Puigcerdà settlement. In the second phase (2015–2016), an additional 15 people were incorporated, although not all of them came from Puigcerdà or any other informal settlements. Consequently, the group was highly diverse in terms of administrative status, language skills, basic needs, and adherence to cooperative values (Labcoop, 2023).

The technical team believed that before officially launching the cooperative, the material needs of the cooperative members had to be addressed. As soon as workers were selected, they were given housing as well as financial and administrative support. In terms of housing, the project involved the provision of public rented housing, but at least in the first phase, this provision was not met due to the scarcity of the Barcelona public housing stock, so they had to turn to the private housing market. In terms of financial needs, members of the cooperative were given a salary, equal to the minimum interprofessional wage, part of which was issued through a social currency to buy basic necessities in stores that the technical team managed to sign an agreement with to be part of the scheme. Nevertheless, many of the workers were dissatisfied with this solution. They argued that the network of shops was not big enough to provide an acceptable degree of freedom in selecting food and other products and that they were often more expensive than other shops. In relation to their administrative status, a collective application was submitted by a team of lawyers, demanding regularisation for 'exceptional reasons' for all these irregular workers. In 2017, 23 out of 30 had been regularised, including five who had already residency permits and 18 who had already begun the regularisation process, while seven others were still waiting for a resolution. The collective regularisation was considered a success, since it was the first time that this type of regularisation had been demanded for an entire collective and not individually (IGOP, 2017).

In parallel to this, Procoop was working with some selected workers to set up the waste-picking cooperative that became operational in June 2015 and took the name of Alencop. Although Alencop was commonly called a waste-picking cooperative, its economic activity was substantially different from that carried out by the same workers when they had performed informal waste-picking. In order to formalise and regularise this activity within the framework of existing rules that consider waste-picking illegal, Alencop provided a free service for home waste collection. Thus, from a legal point of view, waste was freely and spontaneously donated by companies and private individuals to the cooperative. In the first phase, the service was provided only in the Sant Martí and the Sant Andreu districts. It subsequently expanded to the Eixample, Ciutat Vella, Sants-Montjuïc, les Corts, and most of Nou Barris. Once the waste had been collected, it was sorted and stored in a private warehouse. At this point in the chain, the classified waste had to be sold to waste management companies or other recycling companies in the same way as informal waste pickers do. Alencop was not a self-sufficient business and had a very limited turnover. Public resources covered approximately 80% of the business, while only 20% was generated by the activity. The project aimed to achieve a balance where 50% of its economic sustainability would be guaranteed by the cooperative. However, it never managed to do that and continued to require an important economic contribution from the city council.

It was true that the Alencop project represented an innovative policy intervention, and a significant step forward compared to the destructive approach taken with the Puigcerdà informal settlement. However, it did not fulfil its potential to create a rhizomatic urban commons-local state assemblage (Bianchi, 2022a). The cooperative's workers were never granted full self-governing capacity. While decisions regarding the cooperative were officially meant to be made in an assembly involving both the workers and the support team, in fact, this assembly played only a marginal role in the cooperative's management. Most decisions were negotiated between the city council and the support team. Furthermore, the support team handled most of the daily tasks, including managing the public budget allocated to the project, maintaining all of the cooperative's accounts, overseeing bureaucratic and administrative work, and managing business relationships with other partners. This left the workers feeling that they lacked control over the cooperative; this is reflected in what one of the members explained:

> They told us the cooperative was for us, but it turns out that some decisions didn't fit within the cooperative. [...] I was the holder of the cooperative's card, but we never knew anything about the accounts, how much money the cooperative received, or how much it paid out. We were also unaware of the types of contracts the cooperative had; it was a right we had as members, but it was never exercised.
>
> (Labcoop, 2023)

In short, the sub-Saharan members of the cooperative had little autonomy in making decisions about the cooperative's development, and their role was limited to providing labour without being fully involved in the decision-making processes. As one cooperative member pointed out, the lack of opportunities for taking on greater responsibility in managing the cooperative made them feel less like members of a workers' cooperative and more like participants in a social integration scheme (IGOP, 2017).

With the arrival of BComú, little changed in relation to Alencop. The cooperative members still had little say in decision-making, and the cooperative was still heavily dependent on the economic resources of the city council. It was this lack of financial independence that ultimately led the new council to take the controversial decision to dissolve the cooperative. This decision was met with strong opposition from the workers, who, as a result, faced the prospect of returning to their condition of multiple exclusion. They appealed to the city council to reconsider, stating on Facebook:

> An emblematic project that succeeded in dignifying the lives of 30 people cannot end like this; the danger of returning to the settlements is real. Barcelona City Council, which created the cooperative, has a moral responsibility and cannot abandon us now.
>
> (Alencop, 2020)

However, the city council remained resolute in its decision and instead focused on concentrating efforts on a transition plan for the cooperative members. Thus, rather than making real efforts to transform this arborescent urban commons-local state assemblage into a more rhizomatic form, BComú ultimately opted to dissolve it. This move highlights the limitations of the left-wing government in supporting the diversity of urban commons in the city, especially when they require a considerable and constant contribution of public finances. These limitations, however, are evident not only in the management and decisions related to the Alencop cooperative, but also in the management of the continued multiple exclusions experienced by the sub-Saharan immigrants, who were still relying on informal settlements to survive.

During BComú's mandate, in fact, the living conditions of the city's sub-Saharan immigrants remained inadequate, and forced them to find integrated forms of subsistence. After what happened to the Puigcerdà informal settlement, they stopped squatting in large industrial factories in the Poblenou area and began to occupy individual apartments in the peripheral cities outside Barcelona. Located outside the administrative boundaries of the Catalan capital and lacking the critical mass of residents necessary to articulate strong political demands, these occupations were tolerated by the respective authorities as part of a strategy of co-optation and taming. In the years that followed, some informal settlements continued to exist in Poblenou, but involving far fewer people (between 6 and 10 people). The BComú government addressed these occupations in Poblenou by trying to deal with them in a less repressive way, offering social rather than legal solutions. In the end, however, the BComú government did not act very differently from its predecessors. Both residents and activists in Poblenou claimed that if Ada Colau's government had been faced with an occupation like that of Puigcerdà, it would not have been able to prevent the eviction. As one resident noted:

> The BComú government has already had to deal with some cases of informal sub-Saharan settlements, albeit smaller ones, such as in Carrer Pamplona (Poblenou), and in the end it did the same thing its predecessors did.
>
> (Interview)

As one public social worker pointed out, unlike the previous government, which had implemented immediate reactive policies, this administration took time to reflect and plan for the long term. However, there did not appear to be any significant changes in BComú's policies to address the multiple exclusions of sub-Saharan migrants, although there was undoubtedly greater openness and dialogue. As the same social worker put it:

> There are good intentions, and I hope there is more room for manoeuvre, but at the moment (2018) they (BComú) are not brave enough to approach this issue from an alternative perspective.
>
> (Interview)

The policy interventions of BComú, however, evolved over time. Learning from these experiences, particularly from the case of Alencop, its actions did not always result in the creation of arborescent urban commons-local state assemblages, nor in their destruction, as seen in the cases of Alencop and other informal settlements in Poblenou. On one occasion, guided by a supportive rationality, the new administration managed to implement a policy intervention that appears to have led to the creation of a rhizomatic urban commons-local state assemblage through the establishment of the Diomcoop street vendors' cooperative.

During its mandate, BComú had to deal with the problem of the proliferation of informal street vendors. Many sub-Saharan migrants had decided to engage in this informal activity when waste collection became even less profitable, and they struggled to survive below the poverty line. However, as street vending developed in the city's tourist centre, it came under constant media scrutiny and stigmatisation. Ada Colau's administration responded to this situation with a solution that was similar to what had been implemented in the Puigcerdà settlement, creating Diomcoop in 2017. This cooperative offered its members, many of whom had previously been involved in unauthorised street vending, the opportunity to engage in formal employment, primarily in the textile sector, thus providing a sustainable and lasting response to their social and labour inclusion needs.

This cooperative is still in operation and has developed differently from its sister project, Alencop. Although the project was initially heavily subsidised by the municipality, which covered 86% of its total costs, the cooperative has since expanded its activities far beyond the textile sector and is now almost self-sufficient, and in 2023 obtained only 12%–15% of its funding from the municipality. Furthermore, after an initial phase in which technical support was crucial – the technical team provided by Labcoop helped build a sustainable economic model and trained workers to develop their management skills – the cooperative is now mostly managed by the members themselves. It currently has 13 members, including six partners, four workers, and others in training. Although technical support is still available, it plays a marginal role (Labcoop, 2023). This has made the members feel more involved in the management of the cooperative; as one of them put it: 'I feel very involved as a member' (Grupecos, 2023). In other words, although we cannot yet consider the Diomcoop cooperative as a fully developed rhizomatic urban commons-local state assemblage, given the ongoing involvement of the technical team, its development appears to be moving in that direction. This suggests that BComú has had the capacity and political will to surpass the limitations previously demonstrated in managing the self-organising initiatives of the sub-Saharan community.

5.5 Conclusion

This chapter has explored the evolving nature of urban commons-local state assemblages in Barcelona, focusing on the case of the Puigcerdà informal settlement. This settlement, its eviction, and the Alencop waste-picking cooperative serve as compelling examples of how these assemblages can shift between rhizomatic and arborescent forms, or even be destroyed, and how arborescent assemblages can form under both left-wing and right-wing local governments. The circumstances under which the Puigcerdà informal settlement came into being show how rhizomatic assemblages can form under a co-opting and taming rationality, tolerated by conservative governments for economic and political convenience. The sub-Saharan migrants' capacity for self-government developed in the abandoned factory, enabling an integrated form of subsistence that the city council's policy intervention failed to provide to these marginalised and exploited migrant communities. However, this rhizomatic assemblage proved fragile when it became contentious and posed a political risk to the local government. The conservative government's response – evictions and the creation of the Informal Settlement plan – illustrates how, when confronted with the empowerment of marginalised and exploited migrant communities who demand rights and recognition, and challenge established legal frameworks and power structures, the authorities often destroy these assemblages.

The difficulty of engaging with contentious and politically risky commons is evident not only in the case of conservative governments, but also for left-wing governments, which, despite being driven by a more supportive rationality, often seem either uninterested or unable to create rhizomatic urban commons-local state assemblages. The transition from the Puigcerdà settlement to the creation of the Alencop waste-picking cooperative under the conservative government, and its continuation under the BComú government, illustrates the tendency of both governments to favour arborescent assemblages when dealing with marginalised and exploited migrant communities. While Alencop represented a seemingly commons-sympathetic policy intervention that aimed to recreate the previous urban commons-local state assemblage under a different guise, it fell short of granting its members genuine self-governing autonomy. The cooperative's structure, which relied heavily on technical assistance and municipal funding, reflected an arborescent approach that limited workers' decision-making power.

It is also true that BComú's approach also shows elements of discontinuity, as it appears to have succeeded in creating a more rhizomatic urban commons-local state assemblage with the sub-Saharan community through the creation of the Diomcoop cooperative. The development of Diomcoop, characterised by increasing self-sufficiency and member-led management, suggests that left-wing governments can learn from past experiences and create more genuinely commons-sympathetic policies, even for marginalised and exploited migrant communities. Despite this exception, however, the chapter shows how both conservative and left-wing governments have shown a propensity for arborescent structures, sometimes resorting to eviction when faced with contentious and politically risky urban commons. BComú's initial approach to Alencop and smaller informal settlements mirrored that of its conservative predecessors, highlighting the challenges of changing institutional practices and mindsets even within progressive administrations.

Note

1 The 22@ Plan in Barcelona, launched in 2000, was an urban regeneration initiative which transformed the former industrial neighbourhood of Poblenou into a hub for knowledge-based industries, innovation, and technology.

References

Ajuntament de Barcelona (2012a) Mesura de Govern: Pla d'assentaments irregulars. Barcelona.

Ajuntament de Barcelona (2012b) Mesura de Govern: Programa d'Illes Autosuficients de Barcelona. Barcelona.

Ajuntament de Barcelona (2014) Memòria 2014 Àrea de Qualitat de Vida, Igualtat i Esports. Barcelona.

Alencop (2020) *Apoyo a los trabajadores de Alencop*. Facebook. 28 May 2020. Available at: https://www.facebook.com/share/p/183SN89sjH/ (Accessed: 22 December 2024).

Arango J (2000) Becoming a country of immigration at the end of the 20th century. In: King R, Lazaridis G, and Tsardanidis C (eds) *Eldorado or Fortress? Migration in Southern Europe*. London: Macmillan, pp. 253–276.

Bianchi I (2022a) Empowering policies for grassroots welfare initiatives: Blending social innovation and commons theory. *European Urban and Regional Studies* 30(2): 107–120. DOI: 10.1177/09697764221129532.

Bianchi I (2022b) The local state's repertoires of governance strategies for the urban commons: Nuancing current perspectives. *Environment and Planning C: Politics and Space* 40(8): 1784–1800. DOI: 10.1177/23996544221108333.

Dias SM (2016) Waste pickers and cities. *Environment and Urbanization* 28(2): 375–390. DOI: 10.1177/0956247816657302.

Domínguez-Mujica J, Guerra-Talavera R and Parreño-Castellano JM (2014) Migration at a time of global economic crisis: The situation in Spain. *International Migration* 52(6): 113–127. DOI: 10.1111/imig.12023.

Gremi Recuperaciò de Catalunya (2013) *Diagnosi ambiental, social i econòmica de la compra de residus metàl·lics a particulars a Catalunya*. Barcelona.

Grupecos (2023) *Marie Faye: "Cada persona que entra a Diomcoop aporta un coneixement nou"*. Available at: https://grupecos.coop/noticies/marie-faye-cada-persona-que-entra-a-diomcoop-aporta-un-coneixement-nou/ (Accessed: 22 December 2024).

Haan A, and de Maxwell S (1998) Poverty and social exclusion in North and South. *IDS Bulletin* 29(1): 1–9. DOI: 10.1111/j.1759-5436.1998.mp29001001.x.

IGOP. (2017) *Informe ALENCOP 2017*. Barcelona.

Isusi I and Corral A (2007) Employment and working conditions of migrant workers – Spain. EurWORK.

Juzgado Primera Instancia 21. (2013) Juicio Verbal 411/2013 s.c: Desahucio por precario. Barcelona.

Labcoop (2023) *Cooperativisme d'inclusió sociolaboral: aproximació a models d'acompanyament*. Barcelona.

Pradel-Miquel M (2017) Crisis, (re-)informalization processes and protest: The case of Barcelona. *Current Sociology* 65(2): 209–221. DOI: 10.1177/0011392116657291.

Sales Campos A (2013) Las personas sin hogar en la ciudad de Barcelona y la evolución de los recursos de la Red de Atención a Personas sin Hogar. Barcelona.

Vanguardia L (2012) La nave de los inmigrantes del Poblenou se usará para hacer pisos. *La Vanguardia*, 20 July.

6 Conclusion

6.1 Strategies for enhancing the politics of the urban commons

In recent decades, and especially after the 2007–2008 financial crisis, urban commons have emerged in European cities as a repertoire of collective action that fosters a form of antagonistic politics, challenging the neoliberal order and its institutions – namely the state and the market – while offering alternatives in the here and now of the urban environment (Bianchi et al., 2022). Despite their capacity to work towards alternatives, the development of the politics of urban commons can be heavily influenced by the context and the other actors with which they interact, particularly the state and the market. This book has explored the relationships between the urban commons and the state, particularly the local state, with the aim of investigating how these relationships can be beneficial for the politics of the urban commons. In doing so, the book has sought to challenge the two main schools of thought on the commons, the neo-Marxist and the neo-institutionalist approaches, both of which tend to adopt rather siloed and deterministic perspectives on the relationship between the commons and the state. Neo-Marxists typically see this relationship as inevitably leading to co-optation or destruction (De Angelis, 2017; Stavrides, 2016), while neo-institutionalists argue that it leads to support for the commons (Iaione and Foster, 2022). However, this book not only critiques both these positions but also theorises and incorporates the specificities of the municipal scale into the analysis of these relationships, which is another variable that has been overlooked by these two streams of literature.

Drawing on Deleuze and Guattari's assemblage theory (Deleuze and Guattari, 1987), this book has examined the interactions between the urban commons and the local state as assemblages – focusing on relationality, contingency, and agency – and has adopted a less deterministic and more outcome-oriented understanding of how interactions between the urban commons and the local state can benefit the politics of the urban commons. We have done so by assuming that the rationalities adopted by the local state – co-optation, destruction, and support – are multiple, evolving, and

DOI: 10.4324/9781003398493-6

overlapping and may lead to policy interventions that do not necessarily produce the expected outcomes in terms of the politics of the urban commons (Bianchi, 2022c). These outcomes need to be assessed on an empirical basis, as they can take unforeseen directions depending on the context and on the way local state-urban commons assemblages are formed. We have also drawn on another of Deleuze and Guattari's theoretical concepts, namely the distinction between rhizomatic and arborescent assemblages – the former being anti-hierarchical and anti-assimilatory and the latter embodying the opposite – and have used this distinction to assess how the interactions between the urban commons and the local state can benefit the politics of the urban commons. Moreover, we have expanded this analytical framework by incorporating the municipal scale, arguing that while it represents a space of ambivalent political possibilities for enhancing the political action of urban commons (Bianchi, 2024b), it also offers specific opportunities. These opportunities are rooted in the specificities of the municipal scale and its openness to material resources, participation, and radical positionings. Material resources include access to funding, land, and infrastructure; participation refers to the capacity to take part in participatory processes and influence decision-making and governance; and radical positionings reflect the capacity of left-wing actors to gain power and push forward transformative political agendas. These specificities of the local state can be more readily exploited by the urban commons to advance their goals. It is in this sense that we suggest the local state can act as a node of disunity within the broader ensemble of state scales, providing a window of political possibility for the politics of the commons to develop.

The main argument put forward by this book is that urban commons-local state assemblages can be politically beneficial for the urban commons, as long as they work in a rhizomatic manner. These rhizomatic assemblages, in which the local state neither assimilates nor hierarchises the transformative aspirations of urban commons, enable them to maintain their self-governing autonomy while potentially sacrificing some degree of material autonomy (Bianchi, 2022a). This occurs through engagement with the local state, benefitting from its financial resources, logistical support, and legal framework, and taking advantage of commons-sympathetic policies (Bianchi et al., 2022). What this book has sought to understand is how rhizomatic assemblages can form and be sustained over time, and how they can avoid transforming into arborescent structures. In particular, we have examined how local state rationalities and policy interventions can enable the creation of different types of urban commons-local state assemblages, how these dynamics evolve over time in response to power and policy shifts, and how they can vary significantly within the same urban context. Ultimately, this analysis has aimed to understand how urban commons can harness these dynamics and transform them in ways that favour their political objectives.

Building on this analytical framework, the book has examined the case of Barcelona, a city with a rich history of progressive politics and self-organisation. Barcelona's unique socio-political context, characterised by a strong anarcho-cooperativist tradition and a recent surge in urban commons initiatives, provides an ideal setting to explore the dynamics of urban commons-local state assemblages. The study has focused on two contrasting cases that emerged in the aftermath of the 2007–2008 financial crisis: the Can Batlló sociocultural centre and the Puigcerdà informal settlement. These cases, unfolding across different political administrations – from conservative to the New Municipalist government of Barcelona en Comú (BComú) – have offered valuable insights into how urban commons navigate and negotiate their relationships with the local state. By analysing these cases, the book has helped throw light on the complex processes through which rhizomatic and arborescent assemblages form, evolve, and transform, revealing both the possibilities and challenges of enhancing the politics of urban commons through engagement with local state institutions under different political regimes.

Building on these findings, this book has aimed to contribute to a more nuanced understanding of urban commons-local state dynamics, moving beyond the binary perspectives offered by neo-Marxist and neo-institutionalist approaches. Our analysis has shown that the outcomes of urban commons-local state interactions are not predetermined but are shaped by a complex interplay of factors, including the specific socio-political context (crises, moments of political volatility, etc.), the nature of the urban commons in question (whether it is composed of well-educated middle class activists or marginalised and exploited migrant populations), and the strategic choices made by both commons and state actors. The cases of the Can Batlló sociocultural centre and the Puigcerdà informal settlement demonstrate how two urban commons that emerged during the same period, under the same local government, were subjected to very different rationalities and policy interventions by the local state. These differences resulted in the creation of distinct forms of urban commons-local state assemblages. Furthermore, our examination of Barcelona's evolving political landscape, going from a conservative government to New Municipalist politics, illustrates how changes in local state rationalities and policy interventions can create both opportunities and challenges for urban commons. These dynamics underscore the need for urban commons to develop sophisticated strategies of engagement with the local state, using progressive governments' supportive policies while guarding against co-optation or loss of autonomy, but also taking advantage of the material concessions that even conservative governments can offer.

In the following section, we will explore in detail the strategies that urban commons can employ to enhance their political action when they form assemblages with the local state. There are three main strategies, and they are related to the capacity to exploit local state rationalities and policy interventions, the ability to navigate the tension between the autonomy of urban commons and local state support, and the possibility of occupying the local state through New Municipalist platforms.

6.2 Exploiting the local state's rationalities and policy interventions: developing a strategically recalibrated approach to urban politics and building networks with social movements

To understand the complex relationship between urban commons and the local state, we must move beyond seeing local state approaches towards urban commons as monolithic and predetermined, as both neo-Marxist and neo-institutionalist scholars do. In this book, this has meant unpacking the concept of local state 'approaches' into two key components: the rationalities that drive local state action – co-opting, destroying, and supportive – and the specific policy interventions that result from these rationalities. Rationalities represent the underlying logic guiding local state action, while policy interventions represent the way through which this rationality is operationalised. Rationalities and policy interventions need to be understood and assessed within the context of the broader local state urban agenda. A rationality that may appear supportive – because it results in policy interventions that address some of the material demands of the urban commons – may, in fact, align more closely with a co-opting rationality if it is pursued in a context of an urban austerity agenda. One example of this would be the agenda pursued by the conservative government in Barcelona in the aftermath of the 15M, which sought to materially support some urban commons while ultimately aiming to tame and integrate them into a broader governance framework, all within the context of neoliberal fiscal retrenchment. Also, a rationality that may appear co-opting, since it results in policy interventions that can shift the cost of social reproduction onto communities, may align more closely with a supportive strategy, if it is pursued in a context of the implementation of city-wide commons-sympathetic policy and expansive spending. BComú's agenda with Can Batlló is an example of this rationality, as its support for the project led to savings for the New Municipalist government while being pursued within a broader context of expanding public investment and welfare.

But going beyond how we assess rationality and policy interventions, one of the key arguments of this book is that the outcome of local state rationalities and policy interventions can have unexpected consequences for the politics of the urban commons. A co-opting rationality that leads to policy interventions that address some of the material demands of the urban commons in order to calm politically volatile moments may indeed be beneficial to the politics of the urban commons. The case of Can Batlló urban commons illustrates this point. Initially, under the conservative government's co-opting rationality, pursued within an urban austerity agenda, the Can Batlló sociocultural centre managed to leverage limited material support to enhance its political action. Conversely, policy interventions that stem from supportive rationalities can weaken the political action of urban commons. The case of the Alencop waste-picking cooperative exemplifies this dynamic. Initiated under the conservative government and continued by the progressive BComú administration, Alencop demonstrates how policy interventions, despite being moved by a supportive rationality, can eventually lead to rather limited political action.

These examples underline two critical points. First, that the impact of each type of rationality and policy intervention regarding the politics of the urban commons does not depend solely on the rationality and policy intervention itself, but also on the relational dimension within the assemblage – that is, whether and how the urban commons can exploit these rationalities and interventions to their advantage. Second, this capacity for exploitation may vary for each urban commons, depending on its power relations with the local state. Some urban commons, which have less asymmetrical power relations with the local state, can be more capable of exploiting the rationality and policy interventions of the local state – for example, those composed of highly educated, middle-class individuals who do not represent a political risk for the city council, such as those involved in the Can Batlló sociocultural centre. Other urban commons which have a more asymmetrical power relationship with the local state, such as those composed of marginalised and exploited migrant communities claiming their rights, and that represent a political risk for the local state, such as the Puigcerdà informal settlement, can be less able to do so. In these cases, co-opting and repressive rationalities and policy interventions may be quite effective in achieving their objectives (Bianchi, 2022c). The fact that urban commons have different degrees of agency implies prioritising diverse strategies to enable them to proliferate and develop their political action in the city. This is why, first of all, urban commons should understand and assess their capacity for agency and act accordingly.

Urban commons that have more potential agency to take advantage of state rationalities and policy interventions, in order to be as effective as possible, should prioritise developing what we call a strategically recalibrated approach to urban politics. This requires the ability to read and interpret shifting political landscapes, identifying opportunities within various political junctures in order to take advantage of them, such as in cases of weakened state action or heightened social mobilisations, for example, the 15M movement. Additionally, they should understand how to leverage potentially supportive policy frameworks, regardless of the underlying state rationalities or political regimes in place. There is nothing wrong with urban commons taking advantage of the material concessions that a conservative government might offer them in order to pursue their transformative aims, as long as this is done strategically and with shrewd political awareness. To do so, urban commons should carefully articulate their values and objectives in ways that strategically resonate with prevailing policy paradigms and discourses or challenge them productively, while maintaining the integrity of their transformative vision. However, engaging with policy interventions, made by both right-wing or left-wing governments, requires urban commons to remain vigilant and flexible, continuously reassessing their strategies in response to shifting political landscapes. This adaptability is crucial, as government rationalities and policy interventions evolve over time, often in unpredictable ways. This ongoing process of recalibration allows urban commons to maintain their transformative potential while navigating the complex and ever-changing terrain of interactions with the local state.

Urban commons that do not hold the same capacity to take advantage of local state rationalities and policy interventions, since they are subject to aggressive co-opting and repressive strategies, need to go further. Beyond adopting a strategic recalibrated approach to urban politics, in order to defend their right to exist, they should also focus on building strong alliances with more powerful urban commons in the city as well as other social movements and civil society organisations. Such transversal alliances should outline political strategies that push the local state – especially, but not only, if it is governed by progressive forces – to create conditions that will ensure that more contentious and politically risky commons are not marginalised, criminalised, or displaced, but are allowed to develop in the city. This requires activating struggles, as well as challenging existing legal frameworks: questioning what is legal and illegal, what is formal and informal. Power dynamics need to be shaken up to empower marginalised and exploited communities, in terms of agency and resources, and to push the boundaries of what is and what is not considered acceptable in the urban order. These struggles may not produce immediate results, but the gradual accumulation of these efforts, along with bringing issues such as informality within highly marginalised and exploited communities into the public and political debate, may eventually pave the way for these types of urban commons to be recognised as having a legitimate right to exist in the future. Obviously, this network building can also be extremely useful in strengthening the politics of urban commons that have more agency, but it is an aspect that is particularly crucial for those that are less advantaged in this respect.

In short, exploiting the local state's different rationalities and policy interventions means that urban commons need to evaluate their differential power relations with the local state in order to calibrate — and constantly recalibrate — a set of strategies that are not only potentially more effective but also aligned with their capacity for agency and room for manoeuvre. These strategies range from crafting sophisticated tactics for reading political landscapes to exploiting opportunities across multiple, evolving, and overlapping local state rationalities and policy interventions, whether they are pursued by right-wing or left-wing governments. They also involve strategically adapting to existing policy interventions not merely to take advantage of them, but to reshape their impact. They also require network-building with social movements and civil society organisations to collectively challenge and push the limits imposed by the local state or other actors on what is considered possible within the urban order, questioning the frameworks that define which urban commons are allowed to exist in the city and which are not.

6.3 Navigating the tension between urban commons' autonomy and local state support: building both self-governing and material autonomy

Beyond the development of strategies to exploit local state rationalities and policy interventions, there is still a fundamental dialectic for urban commons when they engage with the local state: how can they form assemblages with the local state and use their material resources while continuing to enhance their transformative potential? This dialectic represents a critical challenge for the political action of urban commons, and also requires strategic manoeuvring. In order to analyse this dialectic in depth, in this book, we have unpacked the concept of autonomy, distinguishing between material autonomy and self-governing autonomy. Material autonomy refers to the urban commons' capacity to sustain themselves in terms of financing, property, and logistics without relying on external resources, particularly those of the local state. Self-governing autonomy, on the other hand, pertains to the urban commons' ability to make independent decisions regarding the objectives and scope of their transformative projects. This distinction is crucial because it reveals that urban commons may choose to engage with local state resources in a strategic way (thus partially sacrificing material autonomy) while still maintaining their self-governing autonomy. This is what we mean when we say that urban commons and the local state form a rhizomatic assemblage.

The case of Can Batlló sociocultural centre in Barcelona exemplifies how the dialectic between autonomy and state support can be productively managed through the construction of a rhizomatic assemblage. From its inception, Can Batlló demonstrated a remarkable ability to engage with the local state while preserving its self-governing capacity. Under both conservative and New Municipalist administrations, each with their particular rationalities and policy interventions, the centre managed to secure material support without compromising its independence or political vision. Key to Can Batlló's success has been its strategy of 'friction' with the city council: this means that it maintains a critical stance towards state interventions while simultaneously leveraging them to enhance its political action. This approach highlights a crucial aspect of rhizomatic assemblages: they are characterised not by harmony but by a productive tension that allows for mutual interaction without hierarchical subsumption or assimilation.

However, not all urban commons are afforded the possibility of building rhizomatic assemblages with the local state. Although the Puigcerdà informal settlement developed during the same period as the Can Batlló sociocultural centre, apart from when it was first set up, it did not create a similar rhizomatic assemblage with the local state. These types of urban commons, composed of marginalised and exploited migrant communities, find it difficult to develop their own space in the city, and beyond mere tolerance, neither left-wing nor right-wing governments are willing or able to build rhizomatic assemblages with them (Bianchi, 2022a). The creation of the Alencop waste-picking cooperative further demonstrates this: the cooperative's heavy reliance on technical support and municipal funding resulted in an arborescent structure that limited the workers' self-governing autonomy. This finding highlights the risk that commons initiatives, particularly those formed by marginalised and exploited social groups, especially migrant groups, who cannot rely on established money-making practices, become overly dependent on state resources, potentially compromising their capacity for political action.

To navigate this tension successfully, urban commons must learn about rhizomatic assemblages and about how to build and maintain them strategically, never losing sight of the power relations in place with the local state. Rhizomatic assemblages require commons initiatives to constantly evaluate the terms of their engagement with the local state and assess whether particular forms of support enhance or constrain their political action. This implies adopting a form of selective engagement: rather than accepting or rejecting all forms of local state support, urban commons should strategically choose which resources and programmes to engage with. They should prioritise forms of support that allow them to develop their goals and values while avoiding the ones that might compromise their autonomy. However, as we have seen, there are urban commons that do not have the agency to form rhizomatic assemblages or are not permitted to do so, and even in the case of those that succeed, political changes can still threaten their existence.

This is why it becomes clear that while local state support can be valuable for enhancing urban commons' political action, they should not rely solely on this kind of support. Instead, they should actively pursue strategies for building material autonomy to avoid being overly dependent on the local state (Bianchi, 2022b). To achieve greater material autonomy, urban commons can draw significant inspiration from the rich and diverse strategies adopted by the cooperative movement. Federations of urban commons initiatives offer a powerful strategy for enhancing their material autonomy. By pooling resources and sharing knowledge, these federations can achieve economies of scale that individual commons might struggle to attain on their own. Cooperative banks and credit unions represent another crucial avenue for building material autonomy. By establishing financial institutions that are owned and controlled by commons members, urban commons can access funding and financial services tailored to their specific needs and values. By interweaving these strategies, urban commons can create a robust ecosystem to generate resources and provide mutual support, enhance their collective resilience and reduce their vulnerability in terms of unfavourable local state rationality and policy interventions. Most importantly, this collective ecosystem allows urban commons with greater political strength and social capital to support more vulnerable ones in the city and foster more opportunities for them.

Ultimately, the dialectic between autonomy and support in urban commons-local state assemblages is a challenge to be addressed through the construction of urban commons' material autonomy, but more importantly, it is a productive tension that needs to be managed, particularly until this material autonomy is achieved. Through the ongoing negotiation of this tension, through a selective engagement with the local state, urban commons can maintain their self-governing autonomy and pursue their material autonomy, allowing new forms of urban commons political action to flourish. By maintaining their self-governing autonomy, strategically leveraging state resources when this is beneficial for them and building their own autonomous economic capacities, urban commons have the potential to transform themselves and to develop into a means of fostering progressive social change in the city.

6.4 Occupying the local state: leveraging New Municipalism to extend the politics of the urban commons beyond electoral cycles

The strategy of occupying the local state through New Municipalist political forces represents a powerful avenue for urban commons to enhance their political action. The emergence of New Municipalist movements, exemplified by BComú, has offered a unique opportunity for urban commons to influence local governance and foster more supportive policy environments. This approach transcends mere electoral support, involving active participation in party politics, engaging and shaping the political agenda and governance practices of these New Municipalist platforms in favour of urban commons' political action. The case of Barcelona illuminates both the potential and limitations of this strategy.

BComú's ascension to power in 2015 brought with it a wealth of experience from social movements and urban commons initiatives, informing the development of commons-sympathetic policies (Bianchi et al., 2022). This political shift created a more favourable environment for many urban commons projects, as exemplified by the experience of the Can Batlló sociocultural centre. Under the administration led by BComú, Can Batlló benefited from policy interventions that reinforced its political action. The experience that BComú had in government, however, also reveals the limitations of this strategy, particularly concerning more contentious and politically risky urban commons initiatives. The case of informal settlements and other commons that challenge existing legal frameworks and notions of urban order highlights the constraints faced by even the most progressive municipal governments. Despite the desire to deal with these commons initiatives in a different way, using a less repressive, less criminalising policy interventions, genuine support for such initiatives often proves politically unfeasible, even for New Municipalist platforms. Providing effective support would require redefining and expanding what is possible and what is not possible in the urban order, and this redefinition and expansion, in addition to the difficult legal problems it may encounter, may also face political constraints: opposition parties and the media can use these supportive actions to delegitimise the progressive local government. Therefore, having a New Municipalist government in power does not necessarily imply that all urban commons in the city will be truly and genuinely supported.

Nevertheless, having a New Municipalist government in power does remain far more advantageous for urban commons than having to negotiate with social democratic or right-wing administrations. Even if they are unable to fully support more contentious and politically risky commons projects, New Municipalist local governments can develop commons-sympathetic policies, provide material resources to most urban commons, and develop a governance model based on public-common partnerships (Russell et al., 2022). These are collaborative arrangements between the local state and civil society that change the governance and ownership structure of policy-making practices and public service provision, in such a way that both local state actors and citizen representatives can have an equal say in the decision-making process (Bianchi, 2024a). Moreover, New Municipalist platforms can implement regulatory changes that favour urban commons, legitimise commons principles in public discourse, and gradually push the boundaries of what is politically feasible regarding what is possible in the urban order or not. In addition, these local governments can influence regional and national governments to adopt regulatory changes and supportive policies for the expansion of the urban commons, potentially catalysing more systemic change.

This is why it makes perfect sense for urban commons to engage with New Municipalist platforms. Their commons-sympathetic policies, along with their capacity to implement regulatory and policy changes at the urban level and efforts to push such changes at regional and national levels, can help expand the political action of urban commons beyond electoral cycles and protect against unfavourable electoral outcomes. However, this strategy also carries risks of co-optation, demobilisation, and disillusionment if New Municipalist governments fail to deliver on transformative promises. To navigate these challenges, urban commons must maintain a critical stance and continue to build their autonomy even while engaging with New Municipalist governments. This involves, as we mentioned earlier, developing independent resource streams, maintaining strong connections with social movements and civil society networks, continuously reassessing their relationships with local institutions, and preserving their radical political visions.

In conclusion, occupying the local state through radical progressive political forces such as the New Municipalist platforms offers significant opportunities for enhancing the political action of urban commons, but it is not a panacea. Its effectiveness depends on the specific political context and the capacity of urban commons to navigate the complexities of institutional engagement. When skilfully leveraged, this strategy can create a more favourable environment for the development of the politics of urban commons, especially for creating the material conditions for the development of commons in the face of changing electoral cycles, and potentially catalysing broader social and political transformations rooted in the local dimension and beyond it.

6.5 Avenues for future research

As we conclude this exploration of urban commons-local state assemblages, it becomes evident that the relationship between these entities is far more intricate, complex, and context-dependent than in the theories of neo-Marxist and neo-institutionalist scholars. Our analysis, rooted in Barcelona's rich empirical context and informed by assemblage theory, has unveiled a nuanced landscape where the outcomes of commons-state interactions in cities are shaped by different factors and do not follow any pre-established patterns. The central argument of this book – that urban commons-local state assemblages can be politically beneficial for the urban commons when they are aligned in a rhizomatic manner – demonstrates that while the risk of co-optation or destruction is real, so too is the potential for enhancement and empowerment through strategic engagement with local state institutions. These results and considerations point to several key areas for future research and practice, each of which merits deeper exploration and empirical investigation.

Firstly, the challenge of building material autonomy while simultaneously engaging with local state resources demands further scrutiny. This paradoxical endeavour requires innovative approaches that balance the benefits of local state support with the imperative of maintaining material independence. Future research could explore successful models of diversifying resources, examining how urban commons can leverage local state resources as a springboard for developing autonomous economic capacities. This analysis is especially important for urban commons formed by marginalised and exploited communities.

Secondly, the question of replicating rhizomatic assemblages across diverse urban contexts presents a fascinating avenue for investigation. How can the success stories seen in Barcelona be translated to cities with different and less favourable political, economic, and cultural landscapes? This line of inquiry could involve comparative studies of urban commons in various global contexts, to identify common factors that facilitate rhizomatic relationships with local states.

Thirdly, the capacity of urban commons to challenge and expand the boundaries of the current urban order warrants further examination. This includes exploring how urban commons, or networks of urban commons, can push for legal and regulatory changes that create more favourable conditions to operate in, particularly for more contentious and politically risky initiatives. Research in this area could focus on the strategies employed by urban commons to challenge, negotiate with and influence legal and regulatory changes pursued by local state actors, as well as their efforts to cause shifts in public discourse.

Fourthly, the long-term impacts of New Municipalist movements on urban commons and broader urban politics represent a crucial area for longitudinal studies to be carried out. As these movements evolve and sometimes lose political power, how do their relationships with urban commons change? What lasting effects do they have on urban commons, and on urban policy and politics? Have they been able to build a new paradigm of urban governance based more on public-common partnerships? These questions could be addressed through extended case studies and comparative analyses across multiple cities.

Lastly, developing more sophisticated frameworks for assessing the outcomes of commons-state interactions in cities is essential for advancing both theory and practice. This could involve creating nuanced metrics that go beyond binary notions of success or failure, ones that take into account, like in this book, the complex and often contradictory effects of these interactions. Such frameworks would need to consider multiple dimensions, including the preservation of autonomy, the enhancement of material resources, and the expansion of commons networks.

These research directions not only promise to deepen our understanding of urban commons and their relationships with local states but also have the potential to inform more effective strategies for enhancing both the politics of urban commons and progressive urban governance practices in general. As the urban political landscape continues to evolve in the face of multiple and overlapping crises, this research agenda offers a pathway to reimagining and assessing the place of urban commons as an engine of socio-ecological and democratic transformations. The assemblage frontier between urban commons and local states presented in this book represents not just a theoretical construct but a practical arena through which the role of cities can be redefined to push for these transformations. If this is achieved, it could be a step towards securing more equal, just and democratic futures, or at the very least, a defensive stronghold against the rising tides of right-wing extremism and authoritarianism emerging at the national level across the globe. Much like Barcelona has been in the past.

References

Bianchi I (2022a) Empowering policies for grassroots welfare initiatives: Blending social innovation and commons theory. *European Urban and Regional Studies* 30(2): 107–120. DOI: 10.1177/09697764221129532.

Bianchi I (2022b) The autonomy of urban commons' reproduction in relation to the local state: Between material and decision-making autonomy. *Partecipazione & Conflitto* 15(2): 370–389. DOI: 10.1285/i20356609v15i2p370.

Bianchi I (2022c) The local state's repertoires of governance strategies for the urban commons: Nuancing current perspectives. *Environment and Planning C: Politics and Space* 40(8): 1784–1800. DOI: 10.1177/23996544221108333.

Bianchi I (2024a) The democratising capacity of new municipalism: Beyond direct democracy in public–common partnerships. *Policy & Politics* (published online ahead of print 2024). DOI: 10.1332/03055736Y2024D000000033.

Bianchi I (2024b) The everyday politics of the urban commons: Ambivalent political possibilities in the dialectical, evolving and selective urban context. In: Hamel P and Domaradzka A (eds) *Handbook of Urban Social Movements*. London: Edward Elgar Publishing, pp. 284–300.

Bianchi I, Pera M Calvet-Mir L, et al. (2022) Urban commons and the local state: Co-production between enhancement and co-optation. *Territory, Politics, Governance* 12(9): 1333–1352. DOI: 10.1080/21622671.2022.2108491.

De Angelis M (2017) *Omnia Sunt Communia*. London: Zed Books.

Deleuze G and Guattari F (1987) *A Thousand Plateaus: Capitalism and Schizophrenia*. Chicago: University of Minnesota Press.

Iaione C and Foster SR (2022) *Co-Cities: Innovative Transitions Toward Just and Self-Sustaining Communities*. Cambridge, Massachusetts: The MIT Press.

Russell B, Milburn K and Heron K (2022) Strategies for a new municipalism: Public–common partnerships against the new enclosures. *Urban Studies 60*(11): 2133–2157. DOI: 10.1177/00420980221094700.

Stavrides S (2016) *Common Space: The City as Commons*. London: Zed Books.

Index

FSC
www.fsc.org
MIX
Papier | Fördert gute Waldnutzung
FSC® C083411

Kolibri 360 GmbH
Ferdinand-Jühlke-Straße 7
99095 Erfurt, Deutschland
produktsicherheit@kolibri360.de